THE
VILLAGE
OF MY
HEART'S
MISTAKE

My Family in 1953
IN BACK: me, Mama, Wilfred, Papape
IN FRONT: Ronald and Normand

THE VILLAGE OF MY HEART'S MISTAKE

AN ACADIAN LIFE

DENISE CORMIER

encompass
EDITIONS

Published by EnCompass Editions, Kingston, Ontario, Canada.
No part of this books may be reproduced, copied or used in any
form or manner whatsoever without written permission, except
for the purposes of brief quotations in reviews and critical articles.
For reader comments, orders, press and media inquiries:

www.encompasseditions.com
ISBN 978-0-9877258-4-4

Cataloguing in Publication Program (CIP) information
available from
Library and Archives Canada
at
www.collectionscanada.gc.ca

Ink and pencil drawings by David Abelson (www.davidabelson.com)

encompass
EDITIONS

Dedication

For grandsons Matthew and Mark, who
are precious gifts to me, and in memory of
Normand, a special brother.

Appreciation

It is with great pride that I accept a very small part of the credit for the production of this book.

If not for the labours of my now good friend, Robert Buckland, there would be no book. I am indebted to him for his never-ending patient work as my agent, editor, and publisher at Encompass Editions. Knowing I had no clue about how to write a book, he bravely accepted me as his client. Robert, thank you so very much for your support and encouragement.

I also wish to thank my husband, Gerard, and my two children, Michelle and Gilles, for being there for me on those several occasions when I doubted whether I should go on or not.

The Village

I haven't studied a lot of history but when I think about history, I think about it as water. You can imagine it rushing along like a torrent in some places and in other places collecting in eddies and pools, turning slowly, maybe even backing up now and then. So before you begin this book, be warned that Cheticamp is one of those pools. It's true that Cheticantins have changed since I was a girl—they like to think of themselves as pretty up-to-date now—but they can't change the fact that most of them were born in a fishing village at the far edge of the land. They can't change the fact that Cape Breton is a part of the world that speaks English but a lot of people in Cheticamp still speak French. And they can't change the fact that nobody in New York or Paris or even Montreal looks up when something happens to the Deveaus or the Aucoins or the Chiassons.

Cheticamp was inside the old lands of the Mikmaq, who called it *Aotjatotj*. They say this word meant a fine harbour and there *is* such a harbour between the long island and the shore. They also say the Bretons and Basques were the first Europeans to make use of it. These Bretons and Basques were fishermen just like Cheticantins. They steered their little boats back and forth across the Atlantic and fished those waters for centuries.

Our own ancestors were Acadians, people from France who settled in the part of Canada that pushes out into the northern ocean. As time went by, *Aotjatotj* somehow became *Cheticamp* in their mouths. These poor Acadians hadn't been settled a hundred years when a war blew up on the other side of the ocean and over here a British army beat a French army. After fifty years or so there was more war and the new government got worried the Acadians might be disloyal to the English king since the French had a king of their own. I don't know that these Acadians knew much about kings but they got expelled anyway—to Louisiana and France and other places.

It wasn't thirty years though before a lot of homesick Acadians started drifting back. Two hundred years ago, the same British government gave a group of twenty-six of those Acadian families seven thousand acres along the north-west coast of what is now Cape Breton. That was English Canada but nobody really lived there at the time and it's belonged to us Cheticantins ever since.

It's the sea that has kept us, the sea and what we could grow in the fields between the sea and the timbered hills of the coastline. Gypsum was something we had and for a while some of us were gypsum miners; that faded away after the last war. We've tried hard to be a tourist town since and to some extent we are, but Cheticamp is still a working place, even if there are not so many of us doing the old work.

I was born in Cheticamp in the old Sacred Heart Hospital, now long gone, along with most of the Cheticamp I knew. I was a child of the Deveau and Bourgeois families, the only girl of four children. I grew up along the shore—all of Cheticamp is on the shore—and I loved my village and its people and hoped to die among them.

9

Then, in 1996, when I was forty-eight, I left and would never call Cheticamp home again. That's the story I want to tell you now.

The Secret

 t had been my secret and I was content with it, at least content that it was mine. I never felt that fear they talk about: the panic, the sense of impending doom. On the contrary, a sort of peace descended on me.

Cheticamp. I remember you, every corner of you, though I'll probably never see you again. But when a person looks every day of their life at those few streets and houses, that church, that store, that harbour, that mountain that we just called *the Mountain,* that blue sea that hid the fish so many of our men lived by, a person soaks it up the way those old blotters we used in school soaked up our inky scrawls. There's no rubbing that out.

For the boats, weather changed the sea out of all recognition, and since the sea was half our Cheticamp world, weather changed that world too. The gray of rain went on forever and winter snow storms called up a waste of white beyond the harbour. Those were the dark days. But then, when the clouds blew by and the sun tilted up in the spring,

Cheticamp was all glory: so much sky and so much sea to reflect it and the mountain tipping the earth up behind the village so we could study its beauties from the back steps of our houses.

Such was a particular day in June, 1986—it might have been midsummer day: I'm talking about clean and sharp and warm, all at the same time. We were a hospital, Sacred Heart Hospital, which is why maybe somebody dreamed up the annual Sneaker Day. We'd all put on sneakers and then a dozen or so at a time would go out for an hour in the middle of the workday and walk and talk and chirp like birds freed from their cages. The hospital was by the main road, called the Cabot Trail after John Cabot, who'd once come by this way. It was right down by the shore, but we'd cram into a couple of cars and drive up behind the village to the flat-tish slope at the base of the Mountain. The Plateau, we called it.

We were ten or twelve of us, squeezed into two cars. Marthe Lefort, Gloria Leblanc, Marie Sophie Shomphe, Heather Leblanc were in our car—they were good friends then but much better friends later—and Germaine Campbell was driving. She turned off the main highway and went up Cemetery Road. We were laughing and gabbing like schoolgirls who'd managed to sneak away at recess for a smoke. Actually a couple of us *were* smoking, our cigarettes held outside the car window in the warm breeze. *There* was pleasure: a beautiful day, good old friends, a cigarette, and all that during working hours. Somebody—I can't remember who—started talking about Pauline Q., who'd been seen with Jacques Leblanc at a bar in Margaree Harbour just the week before. Jacques was married to Jeanne, a nice woman who worked at Marie's Salon. We all knew about it but that didn't stop us talking and saying how bad we felt for Jeanne, even though we didn't really know her, and how we all pretty much knew how it would end when she'd married Jacques, who had a reputation for chasing women like Pauline Q. It didn't seem like gossip, really, although I suppose it was. It felt more like the court of public opinion, convened to mete out justice when the real courts would never. A village needs to talk like this because it makes everybody feel better.

"Somebody ought to tell her," Marthe said.

"Somebody ought to tell Pauline's husband," Gloria said.

"He already knows, I bet," Germaine said.

Nobody would tell anybody. The court of public opinion was always called to order in the absence of the accused and the complainant. Only the witnesses attended.

Up on the Plateau, we burst out of the cars. For some reason, even now, I can remember that sun on my face and those sounds that you didn't hear all winter and now they were all around you. Some of the women in the first car had actually started running and were way up the road, which was pretty flat for a stretch. The rest of us walked along, still talking, laughing. After a while, I personally had to stop laughing and after a bit I didn't talk too much but just concentrated on keeping up and even that got harder. The road turned up here, away from the village and the sea and towards the higher slope. The last of our group was way ahead of me now and my steps were getting short and slow. I think it was Gloria who realized I wasn't with them and she turned around.

14

"Denise!" she called. "Denise, come on! Come on!"

I stopped and smiled.

"Something wrong with your sneakers?" Marthe called.

I waved. "No." I couldn't call too loud. "No. You go on. I'm going back to the car. You go on."

The pain, the secret pain. In my chest and up my jaw and out my arms, like a balloon blowing up bigger and bigger inside me. I felt in my pocket for the Tums. They were something I did in the presence of the secret.

I turned and looked back down towards the cars. It seemed a long way but I could manage. I was sure I could. And then all the women from our car were beside me.

"Oh God, Denise," Marthe was saying. She looked shocked and I tried not to laugh. "My God, your lips are blue."

"Yeah yeah," I said. "Never mind that. Go on. I'm just going to go to the car."

"You're going with us back to the hospital," Germaine said. She worked in the x-ray department and lived in Point Cross.

"Denise? Denise?" Gloria was saying, a bit loud, a bit like I couldn't hear her, though I could. I was just looking at a stretch of meadow above us. It was so much like the spot where Mama and I had sat for our picnic.

Refrigerators and Secrets

he refrigerator would arrive on an August day in 1957 quite a few years before the family began to die—Uncle Pierre Paul was the first and he didn't go until 1968—and the excitement of that day melts into the sort of stillness that was Cheticamp. We only had one real street and where I lived it only had houses on one side. The harbour was on the other side. If you stood in the middle of that street on a summer afternoon and turned your head, you could see how it wound way off to the north and south and disappeared in a blue smudge where the hills came down to the sea. If you went up behind our house, there was the forest; it came right down the side of the Mountain and stopped at the meadow.

We were Acadians in Cheticamp and a lot of the Cheticamp men made a living by fishing and farming, especially after the gypsum mine closed. We spoke only French. Everywhere else, up and down the coast, even in Pleasant Bay, the next village to the north, people spoke English and had names like Fraser and Bishop. Maybe that's why we

Cheticamp Acadians were pretty comfortable in our own company. It was that same summer of 1957 that I came across my first English-speaking people, on the lawn in front of the Acadian Inn. An old man in a white hat and his wife in a blue hat stood looking at the spire of the Church of Saint Pierre. They asked me if I lived nearby. I understood and said I did. The man said they found the scenery so beautiful and peaceful, they might move down permanently from the city. I informed him that he was lying and ran home to tell my mother.

Papape had officially announced the refrigerator at dinner two days earlier and I saw Mama watching us for our reactions.

"We won't have to go down to the cold room anymore," she said. "Almost everything will be kept cold right here in the kitchen."

I looked at Wilfred and Normand, but they only nodded and went back to their stew. Even Ronald, who was younger than me, seemed like he couldn't care less, though of course Ronald was always the quiet and agreeable one. Normand was calm and didn't waste words but he could be talkative when he wanted to be. Wilfred, he was the one who enjoyed an argument.

"It has a freezer," Papape said, as though that was nothing much. He glanced at me and I saw his eyes go wide. I smiled and made the corners of my mouth pull down to hide the smile. I knew about freezers: you could keep ice cream in them. Everyone likes ice cream but Papape and I were crazy about ice cream, especially maple ice cream.

He said he'd bring the refrigerator home at six that

evening. I'd figured out that the wait would be a terrible agony and I'd laid careful plans with Georgina the day before. Georgina Aucoin was my best friend. The plan was that I'd be up at eight and have my dolls dressed. She and I would meet at nine and the dolls would have tea before we wheeled them down the lane to Saint Pierre for prayers at ten. Saint Pierre was God's only house in Cheticamp so it was enormous compared to the houses scattered around it, more enormous than the church in any other village (though I'd never seen one), and it didn't surprise me that the strangers who began to appear in the village that summer stopped and stared. Of course they didn't know about our special privilege, growing up right there in the shadow of Saint Pierre. We Cheticamp girls didn't just get to attend mass every morning and twice on Sundays. We didn't just get to listen to the echoes and smell the frankincense and see the sun streaking through the glass saints high above our heads. We also got to use Saint Pierre as our own private chapel—especially important on Saturdays and holidays when all the dolls needed a touch of holy water. And this day, this refrigerator day, would be a perfect time to take them down to the harbour for a swim when prayers were done. They'd only be allowed to watch, of course.

It was eight now and our family had gathered for breakfast. Mama had fried up slices of an enormous ham she'd steamed the day before. She'd poached six eggs so the yolks were hot and thickly runny and in the middle of the table she'd stacked up toast made from her own bread and set down a big mason jar of her own strawberry jam. She and Papape drank tea and Wilfred went down to the cold room to fetch up a creamy jug of the milk Oncle Dominique had delivered from his farm the evening before. I kept looking over at my three brothers. They could hardly sit still during grace, they were so excited about their work on the tree house. They wouldn't be home for lunch because there'd been a terrible encounter between the cowboys and the Indians just a few days earlier and all sorts of important changes had to be made to its defences. Mama had a paper bag ready for each of them: chicken sandwiches and her homemade jam-jam cookies.

At a quarter to nine Papape said goodbye and climbed into the co-op truck—they let him bring it home at night—and left to start his deliveries. Wilfred and Normand and Ronald leapt from their chairs and tore out the door yelling goodbyes at Mama. I finished my egg and kissed Mama and squeezed Michelle and Claire into their buggy and bumped it down the awfully stony path to Georgina's house, which was a nice big house three doors from me.

I always went in Georgina's house by the kitchen door and she and I went straight up to her room because it turned out her dolls had all been misbehaving and she'd had to sit them on her bed and give them a good scolding.

"You can't go to church unless you behave properly," she warned them. "We'll just wait until you do." They didn't dare say anything back and after a moment she tugged at my arm and led me down the hall to Albert's room.

Albert was Georgina's oldest brother but he wasn't home. She opened his door a crack and pointed. There on the dresser was a tiny black velvet box. We looked back down the hall but no one was around so we went in and Georgina lifted the box from the dresser and opened it like you'd open a small black perfect clam. There inside was a ring such as I

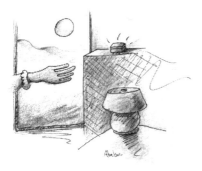

had never seen.

"That's a diamond," she said. "A real one. Albert's getting engaged."

For a long while we stood in awe.

"Can I touch it?" I asked at last.

"No," Georgina said. "It might break."

We passed the kitchen door and Elizabeth, Georgina's mother, looked up. The tub of her washing machine was lurching around in the middle of the kitchen the way washing machines did and there was sweat on Elizabeth's forehead. She had rolled the sleeves of her dress up to her elbows.

"Where are you going, girls?" she asked.

"To church," Georgina answered, not too loudly.

"Church?" Elizabeth had to speak up pretty loud so we could hear her over the machine. Soapy water was splashing out of the tub. "Georgina, you don't have time to go to church. We have to be at Tante Annie Belle's by noon."

Georgina stood there looking down at her dolls, both hands on her buggy handle.

"You should be getting changed," Elizabeth said.

"She can't," I said. I disliked any disruption of plans. "She can't today."

Elizabeth reached down and turned something on the washer. It stopped. She made a little frown. "Why, Denise?"

"The dolls have to go to prayers. They need to."

Elizabeth nodded. "Perhaps they can go tomorrow."

"No!" My face felt red, like it always felt if people tried to stop me. "No, Elizabeth, they must go to confession too."

"Why is that?"

I knew Elizabeth. I knew she was going to laugh in a minute but I didn't know why.

"Because they've been bad. It's important."

She wiped her hands on a towel and came out to the hall. "Denise," she said, "Georgina's Tante Annie Belle is expecting her. You don't want her to make Tante Annie Belle sad, do you? Georgina will get to play with her cousins."

I pressed my lips together.

"Denise." Elizabeth knelt beside me. In fact, she didn't laugh. "There's something you should know about dolls."

"What?"

"They're always blessed. They can be naughty but they can never sin."

"I'll be back at suppertime," Georgina said.

I just glared. It seemed she'd known all along.

I gave the carriage a pretty bad pushing back up the stony path. I let Michelle and Claire bounce on every stone and was sort of satisfied to see them flinging their arms out one way and another. I parked it by the back porch and sat on the stair in disgust. After a few minutes, the screen door opened.

"Are you going to come in and sit with me?" Mama asked.

I took up my place in one of the two rocking chairs and rocked a little but had nothing to say. Mama was folding laundry on the kitchen table. That was the sort of housekeeping she did: the folding, the dishes, making the beds. She wasn't that strong, maybe. When I think of her as she was then, I think of her with a pen in her hand, sitting at the dining room table writing I don't know what, stopping every minute or so to brush her dark hair from her face, looking up at me, smiling. Papape insisted on doing all the heavy work: he washed the floors and ceilings and moved furniture around for cleaning. They did the laundry together once a week.

Mama put the last white sheet on a pile and smoothed it down slowly with her hands. She went out to the cupboard and came back with the wicker hamper.

"I haven't seen many smiles since breakfast," she said.

There are days that sort of crystallize in memory the way sugar sometimes does at the bottom of the syrup jar. It's all the same stuff really, but you can touch the crystals and look at them up close in the sunlight, feel their edges, roll them around in your mouth. I suppose that day was one of those crystal days for me.

We left the house—we never locked the door—and went down the stairs and out the gate. I remember the sun was warm by then and a soft breeze fanned our faces. I don't think I'd noticed either until that moment. We walked together up the dirt road that led to the Plateau. Mama and I each wore a summer dress, hers was light green, mine light blue. We climbed over the fence at the back of Calixte's and at the end of the field cut through a patch of trees we called Le Parque. When we passed through Le Parque we were in the little meadow pretty far up the hill on the Plateau. If you looked back from there you could see all of Cheticamp scattered along the shore and across the blue harbour the fields and forests of Cheticamp Island, the sea beyond. For me, this was like we'd entered another world. Mama spread out the picnic blanket on the grass—the quilt of all colors Mémère had sewn by hand and on her old pedal Singer—and opened the hamper. She'd mixed a jug of bright orange Kool-Aid and buttered some Milk Lunch crackers and stuck them together. She set them out carefully on our plates with two huge red apples I'd been eyeing for days. A wonderful combination.

Everywhere around us were wildflowers and birds. A rabbit hopped by and squirrels made us laugh by leaping between the high trees at the edge of the woods. I could smell the freshly cut hay in the next field and lay back on the blanket and looked at the sky. I was happy, lying there and soaking up the special closeness to Mama, knowing she'd done all this just for me and it was our secret.

The sun had gone down a bit when we started home and

the air was cooler. We stopped to pick a big bouquet of lupins at the side of the path and Mama put a vase on the middle of the table and arranged them carefully, where they didn't wilt for many days.

I carried laundry upstairs and peeled carrots in a basin on the back steps. Twice I went out on the street and looked for the co-op truck, just in case. I took Michelle and Claire up to my room and sat them on my bed, flipped through "Qui me répondra?" which was my favourite book then, brushed my hair, went down and rocked in the rocking chair while Mama was cooking. The kitchen door banged open and Wilfred and Normand and Ronald burst in, all dramatic pantings and exclamations of amazement at their own bravery and were sent upstairs to wash and no buts about it.

I went back out on the street and there is was: the co-op truck was coming, but slowly. By the time it had stopped in front and begun to back towards the house, I was dancing on the front porch, a creature possessed. Papape climbed out of the cab, a tiny smile almost hidden in his broad, handsome face. He came around to the back of the truck without a word and swung open the doors and there it stood, all rounded corners and gleaming white, punctuated by the long straight chrome handle. I was still staring at it when Ernest Bourgeois came over from next door. Papape and Ernest laid some boards from the back to the ground and they struggled together to bring the refrigerator to the kitchen. Even the boys caught the excitement and ran around and shouted at one another and had to be told to stay back or they might be crushed somehow.

Everyone was amazed how the refrigerator fit perfectly in

the kitchen corner, as though it had always belonged there, as someone said. Papape untied the rope that circled it like a belt and opened the door. Everyone went, "Ahh" together.

"Look how clean it is!" Mama said.

"Has it got an engine?" Wilfred wanted to know.

"It's all electric," Papape said. Then he unwrapped the cord and plugged it into the wall plug where the lamp used to go. A busy, quiet hum began and we listened a long moment in reverential silence. When Papape opened the door again, a light magically came on.

Me, I only had eyes for one thing and there it was, refuting all my fears: the freezer compartment. That night, when the dishes were washed and the first food was set carefully on the shiny shelves of the refrigerator and Mama was in the living room reading and the boys were listening to the radio, I went into the kitchen to see Papape putting two little bowls on the table. He didn't say a word but gave me that look and I looked back. Was it possible? He opened the bright white door and then opened the door of the freezer.

"I have three sons and one daughter," he said. He took a box from the freezer. "Some of them love ice cream and some of them sort of like it." He put two spoons on the table beside the bowls. "But I have only one child who really understands about ice cream," he said. He sat down and so did I. "Maple ice cream," he said.

How could a child forget such a day?

Pills

As we walked from the parking lot to the entrance, I told them they were all crazy, wasting such as day. I was okay. They kept looking at my lips. They saw I *was* okay and they looked at one another and then I laughed and then they did too.

A person in my position should not really be taking time off for a sneaker day, anyway. I loved it, walking up on the Plateau, but I was the director of finance for Sacred Heart Hospital and the department had a budget to present the next week. Thirty minutes later I was at my desk when there was a knock and I saw the fingers of J. C. Aucoin's long and unmistakable hand appear around my door as it opened. He was a tall man,

dark-haired and big-boned, famous in Cheticamp for managing to divide himself into Dr. Aucoin, the grave and attentive professional, always to be seen in a suit and tie, and Claudie, the beer-drinking, steak-chomping camper, scuba diver, pilot, motor cyclist, fisherman, hunter and general hell-raiser.

He poked his face into my office. He was a handsome man.

"Denise?"

I set down my pen when I saw his expression.

"Dr. Aucoin?"

"What's happened?"

I looked at him but I had no reply.

"Up on the Plateau?" he said.

"Sneaker day."

"But you've had some trouble."

He came in.

"Yeah, I just got to keep my nose down, Dr. Aucoin. There's a budget due next week."

"But up on the Plateau?"

"Nothing unusual. Who said it was?"

I picked up my pen again. So. That was it. Now everybody knew and my secret was no longer my own.

"I'm okay, Dr. Aucoin," I said. He kept looking at me. "It happens a lot," I said. "I'm used to it."

He shook his head.

"Denise, I want you to stop work and come to my office now."

"I've got that budget."

"Come anyway."

My blood pressure was 160 over 100. I could see from his frown that wasn't good but he hooked me up to his electrocardiogram machine and said the results looked normal.

"You don't feel that pain in your chest and jaw now?"

"No."

"Your arms?"

"No. I'm fine."

He nodded to himself more than to me.

"I'm going to start you on medicine for your blood pressure and we'll run some tests for your blood cholesterol. Also you smoke, right?"

"You know I do."

"How much?"

"About a pack a day."

"I'd like you to stop."

I rolled my eyes. I loved my cigarettes. Everybody knew that.

"And you should lose twenty pounds."

"I don't look bad."

"You know it's your *heart* I'm talking about."

"Dr. Aucoin, I don't see what this heart thing is for me. I'm young."

"How old was Normand?"

"But I'm a woman."

"How old was your father?"

I sat there in the chair and didn't say more.

"I'm going to make an appointment for you to see Dr. Baillie in Sydney. Meanwhile, this requisition is for an

EKG." He scribbled on a paper. "Keep it in your purse. We can't tell much until you have the pain. The moment you feel it, come in. Agreed?"

I nodded.

"And if for some reason you can't get in, I'm going to give you some of these."

He took a small package from the cabinet near his desk. "You know these, don't you?"

"Maybe."

"Normand has them. They're nitroglycerine pills. If you feel the pain and can't get here, put one or two under your tongue and let them dissolve."

"They'll make me better?"

"They'll make you *feel* better."

"That's good. I should get back to work, really."

Saturday mornings I normally went shopping and I'd take the car so I didn't have to carry the groceries home. I'd just turned into the parking lot at the Coop Grocery when I felt the pain. I sat still but it kept growing, filling my chest, filling my arms, pushing my jaw. I opened my purse and looked at Dr. Aucoin's little package of pills, then I put them back and pulled out of the parking lot and drove over to Sacred Heart, about two minutes away.

They put me in a bed in the ER and the nurse went off. She was gone for some time but after a few minutes, I could hear her voice in the next room—not a whisper but low— and the voice of another person.

"I hate to call Germaine," the other person was saying.

"She hasn't had a weekend off for a month."

"Well"—I could hear my nurse—"She's got a requisition from Aucoin so I guess we have to do it."

"Okay okay. I'll call Germaine."

"I'm sorry. I know the whole thing's a waste of time. You know her. She's in finance but she's the nervous sort. She thinks she's one of her brothers. You know them?"

"Oh yeah."

"Anyway, you better call Germaine."

By this point I had the nitro pills out of my purse and two of them under my tongue. I waited for the nurse but she didn't come. Instead, a miracle. The pain disappeared. The pressure inside me dropped away as though Dr. Aucoin himself was right there, doing his magic.

It was quiet in the other room. I got off the bed and stood beside it. Nothing. I gathered my purse and keys and opened the curtain. There was nobody there. I went out without a sound and turned into the hall, walking faster, passed through the main door, cut across the parking lot without looking back, got in my car and started it. I glanced at the harbour, where three kids were jumping off the pier into water that was a lot cleaner than when I'd done the same thing. Not that the kids cared. I could hear them laughing. Maybe this heart business *was* in my imagination—or Dr. Aucoin's. Anyway, I had to finish my shopping.

.

Hot Bodies

here was a knock at the back door and I was always first to jump from my chair and see who it was. A Saturday morning and spring makes a heady combination for any child. Mémère was looking after us while Mama and Papape took a little holiday—they didn't get many. Mémères visits were highlights in our lives. How could it be otherwise when a loving grandmother spent her time baking all kinds of cookies and pies and cooking our other favourite foods and almost no time worrying about what we were up to. When Mama was home she would bake one pie or one kind of cookie or one cake. But Mémère would bake up a storm. She'd have the oven on most mornings and we'd all make pigs of ourselves, then she'd freeze the rest so Mama would have a break when she got home.

It was Georgina at the back door. She was making small urgent gestures.

"What is it?" I had an inkling. I looked back into the kitchen where the boys were already heading up to their rooms on some mission. Mémère was clearing dishes from the table.

"What?"

"We're going swimming at government dock. You want to come?"

Cheticamp harbour was a picturesque environmental hazard that might at any moment offer up sewage, diesel oil or dead fish. For us its turbid waters were a natural playground and almost ridiculously close at hand.

"Maybe. Who's 'we'?"

She made a little face. "You and me."

"It's too early."

"No it's not, Denise. It's warm. And then we could ride our bikes."

These were the years when our dolls were beginning to fade in importance and new companions were entering our lives, the first years of liberation, when we left our corner of the village and took possession of the whole place, even the furthest edges—and not as part of some carefully regulated excursion with our parents, but on our own, the wind whipping our hair and the rubber whirring on the pavement beneath us.

"The bike's broken," I reminded her. My brothers and I shared the old red bike through our childhood, but now the chain was rusted and certain events had delayed its repair.

"Not *that* bike," Georgina said and there was a glint in her eye. "You've got another bike."

Just before Mama and Papape had left, they'd bought Ronald a brand new and terribly shiny five-speed racer. Georgina made no direct reference to it and neither did I.

"Where do you want to go?" I asked.

"We could go to Point Cross. We could go see Tante Marie Flora and see what rug she's hooking."

I may have looked at her the way children do, blankly deciding according to my own self-interest, not trying to hide that.

"The boats will be coming in early this afternoon," she reminded me. "The water's calm today."

"You sure?"

"Sure I'm sure. So after bikes, I'm going down to the factory."

"Are you?"

"You coming?"

I looked back into the kitchen.

"I can't. Mama'd kill me."

"How will she know? She's away."

"My shoes. She'll smell my shoes like last time."

"Last time" referred to one of the biggest lobster feasts ever. I was not the ringleader on that occasion but I'd served the cause with typical enthusiasm.

"She couldn't get the smell out, remember? She had to throw my shoes *away*."

"So don't get in the bin," Georgina advised. "Someone else will."

I shot another guilty look back into the house.

"Okay," I said. I got my bathing suit and towel and we walked across the road and down to the government wharf. Marcel and André were there.

"Don't pay any attention to them," I said.

"Hey Georgina! Hey Denise!" André called. He was a skinny kid. "It's too cold for you! You'll get cramps!"

"See?" I said to Georgina.

"Hey Denise!" Marcel called to me. He was fooling around with an old tire. "Hey, how come you girls wear bathing suits like that? How come you don't wear ones like we got?"

"Let's go in over there," Georgina said.

"Hey, you used to wear bathing suits like ours, didn't you?" That was Marcel again.

"I like it over there," Georgina said, her voice all ice.

"Me too," I said.

It was a blue-sky day and now the sun rose above the mountain behind us and spread across the water to the island. It may not have been the cleanest harbour in the world but it was all ours and on a day like this, with the surface flashing and the island stretched out lazily in the yellow morning light, it was enchantment to me.

We walked back to my house and I was surprised to discover no sign of my brothers. The five-speed was resting against the front porch and seemed to gleam brighter than ever.

"I'm going to go get my bike," Georgina said. That's all she said. She started up the hill. I went in the back door.

"Hello, Denise," *Mémère* said. She was ironing Papape's white shirts for him while he was away. He only wore them to church. She dipped the collar into the starch jug and ironed it again and again until it was as stiff and straight as a wimple. Except for the thump of her iron, the house was silent.

"Are you having a nice day?" she asked me.

"I am, Mémère."

"Would you like a cookie or is it too soon?"

"Can I have one when I come back in?" I asked. I was thinking lobster.

Outside again, I examined the five-speed without actually touching it. There was certainly no harm in looking. I took note of the boy's crossbar across the middle. That was no mystery to me: the old bike had the same crossbar and we'd all used it forever. In fact, except for the funny brake things on the handlebars, the five-speed was a lot like the old bike, except it was shinier and redder and newer and more beautiful.

Georgina growled her tires to a stop on the gravel.

"Ready?" she said.

There are just a few moments there—between the sound of Georgina's wheels and our passing the first intersection—about which I don't have a precise recollection. I was looking at Ronald's new bike and then—perhaps this was one of its many features—I was riding it.

We went down the gentle slope to the main road and through Cheticamp to Point Cross. I pedaled carefully and played with the gear lever. At one point my legs spun fast and easily and the bike went so slowly I almost fell. At another point, I had to stand up to pedal, although the road was almost flat. Within a few minutes, though, I was an accomplished and confident cyclist.

We pulled up at the little store at Point Cross and I dragged my feet to slow the racer to a stop. I was twelve now, tall and skinny, and could reach the ground easily.

"I thought you would go faster," Georgina said. "What time do you think it is?"

I looked at the sun, which was straight above the spire of St. Joseph's.

"Ten thirty."

"On no!" she cried. "We're going to miss the lobster, Denise!"

"Omigosh!" I shouted back.

"Omigosh! Omigosh!" she echoed, laughing. "We've got to hurry!"

I pushed off and struggled a moment with the gears, then we were away, along the curving road and down the hill towards my house. For the first time, I entertained the thought that Ronald might not approve of my borrowing his bike. Certainly there was no time to be lost. I pedaled harder. As we neared my house, Georgina sped by.

"I'll be there in a minute!" I called.

"When?"

"After I park the bike!" In exactly the spot I'd found it.

I seemed to be going awfully fast. In a spurt of panic, I pedaled backwards to apply the brakes but the pedals spun uselessly in that direction. I pulled on the gear lever as I bumped onto the grass uphill from our house. The bike slowed but too little too late. I saw with horror that I would hit the porch but in that moment I remembered to clutch the hand brakes. Fortunately I missed the porch. Unfortunately the big oil tank was just beside the house but fortunately I missed that too. Unfortunately I hit a pipe that connected the oil tank to the furnace.

It was not much of hit—not enough to throw me over the handlebars—but enough to administer a shock. For a long moment, Ronald's new five-speed stood still and I sat still on it and then together we slowly keeled over. I put out my foot and dismounted. I held the handles gingerly, my heart suspended, and I dared to look. Astonishingly, there has no destruction, the wheel not even bent. A wave of relief washed over me. I'd been spared. I walked back to the exact spot where Ronald had parked the bike and leaned it just so, as he'd leaned it. I thought the safest thing at that moment was to go inside and say hello to Mémère but as I went up the steps, I glanced back at the oil tank and saw the oil that was running out in a steady stream.

The man from Irving Oil was calm and soft-spoken, as though he'd been properly trained to deal with girls who had driven their brothers' new bikes into oil pipes. He tightened up the connection in a few minutes and said the company would send a bill. Mémère, who'd looked on, went back to the kitchen.

The repairman gathered his tools. "Do you know where the well is?" he asked. I felt an awful apprehension as I pointed to the little peg that marked the wellhead nearby in the yard. He nodded gravely.

"Pretty near," he said. "I hope that oil doesn't reach it." Then he was gone.

I kept his speculation to myself but for the week that followed, I woke early every morning to be the first to taste the water.

Papape wasn't a fisherman so my life then wasn't all about fishing as it would later be. A lot of other Cheticamp families depended on the sea. The husbands and fathers and brothers went out in wooden boats that were generally not more than about twenty-eight feet long. We called them pic-a-pac boats because of the noise their engines made. When you were in bed at five in the morning and you woke up, you could hear the gravelly pic-a-pac chorus as they headed out.

July and August was the cod season. The men caught the cod with hand-line jiggers and they'd gut each fish by hand and then when they were safely home they'd unload the catch at the process-ing plant about a mile from our house. It was a hard, demanding trade carried out on a some-times hostile sea. When cod jigging ended in the fall, mackerel season began the end of September and continued all of October. November and December was cod-trawling season and the fish were plentiful and big.

May and June were special. They were the lobster months and there was no quota on the number of traps a fisherman could have. Some had as many as four hundred, all made at home and baited with squid. The lobsters met their end in huge cauldrons of boiling water inside the lobster factory. When they were cooked, men and women inside the factory scooped them out and took off their claws and tails for shipment. The rest—the bodies we called them—were dumped still steaming down a chute into the big bin outside.

"Hurry!" Georgina called.

We ran down the hill and along the main road to the factory. There wasn't a moment to be lost because there was only room for about ten kids around the bin. The unwritten law was that if you weren't there on time, you had to hope for another day.

We rounded the corner. There were already four feasters in place, including Marcel and André. They were laughing and slurping, their hands already sticky with lobster and the bin was still steaming from the last batch unloaded. We took our places and I reached in for a hefty lobster body for Georgina and one for myself. We'd got pretty good at using our fingers to scoop out the sweet, steaming green paste tucked up in the front of the shells, then sucking the insides from the four little legs on either side of the body. We had no butter or salt or bibs or napkins and the juices ran down our arms and into our clothes, but we loved our lobster bodies, all of us. Let the stores sell their claws and tails. We were in heaven with as many mouthfuls of lobster as we wanted.

Ten more kids. Now the excitement rose amidst some grumbling and complaining. Those already in attendance reached in deeper to secure their next portions, lest the supply from inside the factory dry up. The lobsters dumped first were pretty far down now.

"Denise," Sylvia said. "Get in and pass out the rest."

"Noph," I protested. My mouth was full. "I went in lafft time."

"Go on, Denise!" Marcel said. "You're good at it. Go on!"

I knew they were playing on my impulsiveness but I didn't really care. I *was* better at it and besides, the brave volunteer who climbed in the bin was guaranteed the choicest portions.

"Go on!" Paul called.

In I went with several encouraging boosts from behind, and my shoes crunched the big brittle shells beneath my feet.

"Pass them, Denise! Hurry!"

"Okay! Wait!"

I plucked up a few beauties and passed them out and was reaching for a monster when I lost my balance and went down hard on the sharp shells and into the slurry of juices.

"Hurry, Denise!"

As I struggled to regain my footing, my flowery cotton dress soaked, I noticed a sudden silence, then other, deeper voices.

"Hey, you kids! Look out! Look out! Get out of the way!"

"Denise is in there!" Georgina shrilled. "Denise!"

I stood up and looked over the top to see the wooden window above the chute was open. I boosted myself up to the rim. Several loyal supporters reached out for me while others danced away. We scrambled from the bin in time to avoid a cascade of hot bodies, a steaming avalanche of lobster, more than all of us could ever eat.

Sixteen throats opened with shouts of triumph.

Opinions

r. Baillie was looking down at me and I was looking up at him. He was a slim man, not too tall, perhaps forty, with a head of curly, tightly clipped red hair.

"How do you feel now, Denise?"

"I'm fine. I'm fine. I just need my nitro."

He nodded. "I know," he said. "But we've got to find out what's happening in there first. That's why Dr. Aucoin wanted you to come to Sydney."

"It's angina. That's what he said it was. Probably angina."

"I'm sure Dr. Aucoin's right. But the nitro won't just make you feel better. It'll make the EKG look better. Appearances aren't everything."

"I know, I know. It would be bad to look good."

"Bad if you *do* have angina."

"You said I did."

"We're trying to be sure, Denise."

A nurse came in and spoke to him. He glanced at his watch and hurried out. I looked around at the curtained cubicle. It wasn't like I didn't know the Sydney cardiac ward—I was my father's daughter and my brothers' sister—but this was my first time here on my back in a hospital bed, the way I'd seen them so often.

The nurse came back, a pleasantly plump light-haired woman with greenish eyes and matching eye shadow.

"I'll be looking after you," she said while she was looking after the machines.

"Hi," I said.

"This is your bell button. You push here if you have pain. I mean actual pain."

Of course I would have pain. I had pain every day now, no matter what I was doing. I had pain walking down the street, sitting at my desk, doing the dishes, lying at home in my own bed.

"I'm okay," I said.

"I'm sure you are. You've just got a case of the nerves, haven't you?"

That was a fine thing to say. Hadn't she heard Dr. Baillie?

"Anyway, that's your bell," she said and she went out.

I looked at my watch. It was almost eight. I'd normally be sitting with the kids at the dining room table, helping them with their homework. Michelle would be writing her exams the next week. I couldn't help anyone where I was now. I lay still and shut my eyes. At least cardiac wards were pretty quiet places. That was a good thing you could say about them. Just a few beeps here and there and a bell somewhere far off. Too quiet, maybe. I wished Michel could be with me, but he couldn't of course. It was June and he was out at sea. I thought about Michelle and Gilles again. It would be nice to talk to them by phone but there didn't seem to be a phone. Still, I knew they were in good hands with Michel's sister, Marie Luce. I started to feel a bit sleepy.

The pain woke me about eleven, filled up my chest and pushed into my arms. This was its usual trick. I reached for my nitro bottle, which I kept by my bedside table. It wasn't there. I sat up with a start. The pain got worse and I saw I was in a hospital ward and it was dark. I grabbed at the bell cord and pushed the button. No one came. The thing was broken. I pushed it again and again, trying to bring it back to life. I could die, Dr. Baillie had said, I could die while I was having this pain. What had they done with my nitro? I pushed the bell again and again.

The nurse switched on the light by my bed.

"Will you please stop that!"

"I've got the pain," I said.

"Where's the pain?"

"In my chest and down my arm."

"Show me where."

The curtain opened and another nurse looked in. She was hardly more than a girl.

"She says she's got chest pain," my nurse said.

"We're supposed to do the EKG," the girl said.

"Tell Randy," my nurse said.

"I need my nitro," I said.

"Tell Randy," my nurse said again.

I already had wires stuck all over me and now a tall young man with acne scars came in pushing a contraption about the size of Mama's old-fashioned washing machine. This was the electrocardiogram equipment I was to meet so often again. The man put some wires into some holes and there was a little hum and he pulled the wires out again and folded them up.

"Can I have my nitro now?" I asked.

"The nurse is looking after you," he said and he went out.

For the first time, I was scared. My heart had been sick for a long time and I'd come to realize it was nothing to ignore. But I'd never been scared, not really. My pain had always been part of my everyday, normal life. It wasn't like this.

Suddenly Dr. Baillie was there and I felt a rush of relief. He was holding a strip of paper.

"Denise?" He kept his voice down. "This won't come as any great surprise. It looks like unstable angina."

I tried to laugh. "I'm usually pretty stable."

"I'm sure that's true—and you'll need to be because this is serious."

He showed me the strip of paper printed by the EKG machine. The line of my heart looked like some sort of musical notation.

"See these shapes here? We call them inverted Ts. They mean your heart's not getting enough oxygen." I took a deep breath. "It's just not getting through and that's why it hurts you."

"Does that mean I can get my nitro pills back?"

He smiled. "Hey, we'll do better than that here. I'm going to put some morphine in your IV. That will ease the pain but it'll also help protect your heart from damage during this angina attack. Also I'm going to put you on oxygen. That'll really help."

"Bless you."

"Have a good night, Denise."

"I'm sure I will."

He went out and after a few minutes the nurse was back. She connected the oxygen tank to the mask and fitted it over my face.

"It's all going to be fine now," she said.

"I know that," I said. My voice sounded funny inside the mask. I'd never had oxygen before. If I'd ever thought about oxygen, I'd thought about taking a big breath of morning air from my porch overlooking the sea.

Concerning Fish and the Man

heticamp, I remember you well. You weren't really a lonely island of French speakers in that sea of English-speaking Cape Breton. Not really. You were the grandest of all the French villages along the western shores of Cape Breton—the capital city of our Acadian world. We Cheticantins had the only church in the region *and* the biggest school, École N.D.A. The unfortunate children of Pleasant Bay, Belle Marche, Petit-Tang, Plateau, and Point Cross, when they outgrew their schools by grade seven, had to take a bus every morning to our big school on the main road of Cheticamp. And among those newly arriving outsiders was a boy named Michel Poirier and sometime after I turned twelve it became clear to me—vaguely at first and then with gathering certainty—that he was my destiny.

We girls faced our sixteenth birthdays with a mixture of excitement and dread. At sixteen, after several years of vague anticipation, you could go to dances at Le Centre Acadien. If some nervous boy had asked you, your evening was made.

If not, you sat on one of the chairs along the wall of the hall and waited.

I was not at all unlucky in the dating game but my sense of incompleteness was oppressive. It was already obvious to me that I would never know happiness until I was with Michel Poirier. He was older than me—two years as it turned out—and he bore a seemingly remarkable resemblance to Adam, the eldest and most serious of the Cartwright sons on *Bonanza*. He was dark-haired like Adam and ridiculously handsome in my eyes. By eighteen he had dropped out of school but, since Fate clearly intended to intervene on my behalf, he found work at the Cheticamp Fish Plant, not a mile from my house. I'd often see him before the lights went down at the Evangeline Theatre or at Le Centre Acadien (our restaurant, our ten-pin bowling alley, our general gathering place) but—the frustration was misery—he remained oblivious. Infuriatingly, I had no trouble attracting the attentions of the pleasant but unmagical Bernie and the light-hearted but eventually tiresome Yvon.

For all of us, childhood was receding now. We'd left our dolls alone in our bedrooms so often, they'd transformed themselves from beloved friends to sentimental ornaments. It was our bikes now and the wind in our faces and bruised knees and scratched legs, whisking through Cheticamp and up the hill to the highlands, parking, laughing, walking the trails alone for hours. With time the bikes were transformed in turn into means rather than ends and they carried us the seven miles to Sunday afternoon ball games at St. Joseph du Moine, where fly balls and catchers' signals were the cover for watching boys.

Bernice was my best friend now. Not that dear Georgina had vanished from the Earth, but it's in the nature of young friendships that we grow by exploring first one, then another. Bernice was my dark-haired second cousin and we were inseparable after school, needing every minute to compare notes on the shifting web of attraction and indifference. The one subject I was careful not to discuss, not even with Bernice, was Michel Poirier. I was young but a certain tendency to determination had only strengthened with time.

It was a spring afternoon in 1964—of course it was spring—and we were together at Le Centre Acadien sharing a plate of French fries. We must have lapsed into a temporary silence. I remember I was watching two bowlers, a couple I vaguely knew.

"Michel Poirier asked me out," Bernice said.

Her voice was a bit muffled because she was biting into her fries as she spoke and the young woman was bowling a strike at that moment. I remember the clatter of the falling pins. A weird prickly sensation passed over me.

"Who?"

"You know Michel. Black hair. He works at the plant."

"Oh sure. Yeah."

"He asked me out to a movie."

"You going?"

"I dunno. I said I'd call him in a day or two."

She snorted—a little rush of laughter as though she were shocked and perhaps pleased at her own nonchalance.

"Oh." I took a bite of the fries. My heart was already breaking.

"I don't know if I really want to see that *Viva Las Vegas* again," Bernice said. "He's boring, anyway, Elvis." She bit off some more and chewed with gusto. "I like the Beatles."

I tried unsuccessfully to swallow. "I wouldn't go," I lied.

"You don't like Elvis either, do you?"

"No. I mean that Michel."

Her eyes were wide. "What did you hear?"

"I heard he's mean," I lied again.

"Really?"

"Lots of people say that." I could hardly believe these were my words.

"You mean, mean to girls?"

"Yeah."

"He sure is quiet."

"Yeah," I said.

"I didn't know he was mean."

"Me neither."

Bernice shrugged. "I don't care about him anyway." She popped the last fry in her mouth. "He's just a fish plant guy. I have plans of my own, like moving to Toronto instead of spending the rest of my life in this place."

I felt almost torn in two by the pulls of joy and indignation. Just a fish plant guy, indeed.

In June of that year, Michel Poirier knocked on the door of our house and stood waiting for me on the step.

"Would you like to see a movie Saturday?" he asked.

"Sure," I said. I stood there. "When?" I finally asked.

"Seven."

"Okay."

When he was gone, I paced my room in a daze. As a result

of my own scheming, there was no one I could immediately share my news with, but this could hardly mute the exhilaration that was trilling away inside me.

He was a shy boy, and quiet certainly. I was Denise, armed—bustling—with self-confidence, talkative, undaunted (as I thought) by the world and the people who inhabited it. Nothing was impossible for Denise. She had simply to will it and even Michel Poirier would ask her out. It had only been a matter of time.

I was drawn by a sort of fascination to this young man, my very opposite, so seemingly strong and capable, yet so timid and retiring. In Cheticamp, dating couples attended mass together on Sundays and I, who was so proud to be seen with my young man, was astonished but compliant when he insisted that we sit at the side of the church and towards the back. When we were alone and he spoke, which was not as often as I hoped, he never spoke of himself. He was, in some way I couldn't quite fathom, a private person. A young woman wiser than myself might have observed that he was especially private in respect to *me*, who had progressed with the months from his date to his girlfriend. When he approached a boat captain to join the crew on a trial run, he didn't tell me about it. He was soon recognized as a natural fisherman and welcomed as a member of the fishing fraternity, but I was the last to know. On a trip to Halifax he had his own name tattooed on one arm and showed it off around Cheticamp; I saw it only when it was healed and already old news. None of this mattered, of course: he was the fulfillment of all my romantic dreams and nothing could spoil my triumph.

The following year brought a surge of excitement to my circle. We were all of us —Honorine, Diane and me— finishing our Grade Eleven in June. You didn't need your Grade Twelve to take an R.N. course. Everyone was talking about the school of nursing in Antigonish. We had to enrol. Honorine said she wanted to be a nurse in Sydney. Diane was hoping she would get a job at Sacred Heart Hospital in Cheticamp. Nervous laughter and conversation surrounded the whole business and I suppose it was my silence that drew attention.

"Denise? What is it?" Diane was looking at me. We were of course in Le Centre Acadien.

"It's nothing."

"Yes it is. Don't you want to go?"

"Of course. But you have to remember my problem."

All eyes turned to me.

"You know about my homesickness. Remember when I went camping with the Bourgeois' and started throwing up so bad they had to rush back to Cheticamp with me?"

"Denise! No! You're not afraid of anything."

"It was a sickness."

"But that was a hundred years ago. You were ten or something."

"I spent days in the hospital on an I.V."

Their faces fell. "Wow." Honorine shook her head slowly in loyal compassion. "That's right."

I let it sink in.

"I'm going anyway," I said finally. "A person like me can get over homesickness."

This last statement at least was true. But when I lay in my

bed that night and half-listened to the melancholy sound of the lighthouse fog horn, I considered what might be at stake. When we put our applications in the mailbox three days later, mine went in last and slowest. At least there were three of us. One of three might easily be rejected and a true friend such as myself could then decline out of solidarity, could she not?

Two weeks went by and I grew weary of talk of nursing. Honorine and Diane were at a pitch of excitement and fear until the morning all three of us received envelopes from Antigonish. All three accepted. All three to move away and train and make careers in the bigger world. Our families were overjoyed and I rewarded everyone with a smile. Perhaps, I considered, a nursing position would open up in Cheticamp. Still, the risk. I had to consider the risk.

F. J. Aucoin's Variety Store stood on the Cabot Trail Highway that ran through Cheticamp and if it had not existed it must immediately have been invented. Where else could a young person buy clothes or dishes? The kindly Freddy Aucoin, proprietor, had provided me with a job as a clerk the previous summer. Now, as the summer progressed and so shortened day by day, I grew unhappier. Finally, I confessed my dilemma to Freddy one afternoon when the store was empty, confessed to the extent that I blamed it on my awful tendency to homesickness, a malady I'd almost succeeded by then in bringing back to life. When I was done, he thought a moment.

"I can't tell you not to make a career, Denise, but I'm sorry to see you so unhappy. I won't hide the fact that you'd make a great employee here at the store. If you do decide to stay, I can offer you a permanent job."

I went home that night and locked my bedroom door and wrote to the good people at the Antigonish School of Nursing.

Mama and Papape were disappointed but when Wilfred came home from McGill University that fall, he was furious.

"You'll never amount to anything!" he shouted, his own disappointment masked with anger.

"Wilfred," Mama finally said. "That's enough. "We can't know who will amount to something and who won't."

"It's stupid," Wilfred growled. He was going up the stairs. "Homesickness. I don't believe it."

He was always smart, that Wilfred, but he had to return to Montreal and take his insights with him. Honorine and Diane went to nursing school and I settled down in Cheticamp to wait. There was only the matter of filling the time. Mathematics had been my strongest subject in school so I ordered accounting books one after another and studied at night. As chance would have it, Freddy Aucoin's bookkeeper retired and I took over her place temporarily, then permanently. Since he also owned the Imperial Garage and its associated heating oil business, I took over the accounting there too.

Tante Marie Stella and I went to Sydney to buy the material for our dresses on a sweltering July day in 1967, two months before the wedding: white satin for me and a light green for her to complement her jet black hair. We each sewed our own dress. I had asked Tante Marie Stella and Oncle Louis Leo to stand for us because I couldn't bear to choose between my brothers. Michel's niece, Rachel, would be our flower girl.

The fourth of September, 1967 was a wonderful day in Cheticamp, exceptional in every way. Everyone was agreed on that. The air was bright and clear, the sun warm, the sea as calm as a pond. Wilfred drove Papape, Mama and me in his new red sports coupe and Papape walked me up the aisle of the old church that had been my neighbour for nineteen years. As we walked together, I looked over at him and saw his face in profile, looking just as it had one Saturday three years before, on the road to Margaree.

That earlier summer had been the summer of the driving lessons with Papape, the highlight of my days. At sixteen, every Cheticamp teenager was expected to leave behind their bicycle and sit behind the wheel of a powerful car and learn about clutches and gear shifts and how to put gas in the tank. Later we would be expected to drive on our own and turn onto the highway and lay full claim to adulthood, even if it were just for an hour.

But the miserable fact was that there could be no lessons for this particular week because Papape and Mama were leaving the next morning for a camping holiday. The house was half turned upside down with their preparations. After lunch, I washed some dishes and moped around from room to room in the slightly lost manner of any disappointed sixteen-year-old. Papape put his head around the corner.

"I think it's time for our drive," he said.

I backed out of the driveway and turned down to the main road. From there we would head north towards our usual practice run along the National Park highway.

"No," Papape said. "Go left today."

I didn't ask him where we were going or why. It was enough to hold the steering wheel of our Viva in my hands and revel in its power. Short as the lesson must be, even these few minutes would be precious for me. We talked as I drove—about their camping trip and about the holy rule that I was not to fight with my brothers while they were gone—while I waited for his instructions to turn around. Instead, we left the Cheticamp highway and followed the broad parkway up into the high Margaree region, then left the parkway for a series of twisting, turning roads, wide fields on both sides, forests between those fields and green mountains above.

An hour had gone by since we'd left home. When finally Papape instructed me to park at the foot of a long meadow, I jumped out to stretch my legs but saw him opening the trunk. He took out two big old cooking pots.

"I wonder what the strawberries are like, after that rain?" he said.

At sixteen a person is still enough of a child to thrill at the prospect of picking strawberries and I was never again to see such enormous berries growing wild. As each plump fruit fell from its tiny plant into my hand, I grew more focused, more transported, more light-heartedly obsessed.

"Don't go too far!" I heard Papape call and looked to see him resting, far down the meadow. I waved. A pair of deer passed between us as though we were not there. The sun began to decline. Two hours passed.

I turned the car back down towards the coastal highway. I had then—for the last time in my life—that sense that God had reserved an afternoon especially for my father and me, as He had once done for my mother and me. I glanced over at Papape as he sat beside me in the passenger seat and I saw his face in profile and he was very slightly smiling.

Now I looked at that face again, as we approached the front of the church. I could see his pride and happiness and I thought I saw something else. Was there a tiredness that had crept over him without my noticing in all the excitement of the months past? We stopped before the rail, our family and friends behind us. He hugged me and gave me a soft kiss on the cheek. I looked at him again but whatever trace of weariness I'd glimpsed was gone, leaving only his smile.

Some people cry when bad things happen to them. I never did, but I couldn't help crying now, despite every effort to hold my tears. I looked over at Michel and at that moment I was sure I was the luckiest woman in the world. I had the man and I had a home.

It had been a condition of my accepting his proposal—my only condition, I might say—that we would have a house of our own. I had not remained in Cheticamp to live with my parents or his, and this he understood. On a Saturday morning that spring, he'd picked me up and we'd driven along the main road of Cheticamp for about a mile. There, in a cluster of five houses, old-fashioned but dignified, stood our house: a veranda the length of the front, wood shingles painted light green with white trim. It's porch was actually a pantry, or rather its pantry was actually a porch, but one with cupboards and a counter for preparing meals. The kitchen and bathroom were large, the living room comfortable and I could picture the spare room beside it as an office for my bookkeeping business. There were three bedrooms upstairs that you could imagine children growing up in. All the ceilings were varnished hardwood. The harbour was at the bottom of the street so Michel would be able to walk home if his boat came in at night.

My new husband was too shy to face a public reception and he probably knew himself best in that regard. I found out much later that he'd been so nervous that morning, Tante Marie Stella had given him a Valium so he could go through with it. In deference to the groom's nerves, then, we held the party at my parents' house and the Deveau women roasted turkeys and cooked potatoes and vegetables with plenty of stuffing and salads and wine to round it out.

58

I looked around. Patrice, Michel's brother, was sitting on the sofa with his wife Gladys and the priest, Father Harland D'Eon. Patrice had everybody laughing with his stories about his trout fishing trips. I saw Tante Bernadette and Tante Marguerite Marie and Elizabeth bringing food in from the kitchen. There was poor dear old Lucie sitting in Papape's La-Z-Boy chair, looking like it was already nap time. Since there were only two tables, they couldn't seat everyone at once and some guests stood smoking outside, enjoying the weather; others were eating, others just gabbing in the living room. Outside, the

girls were waiting for me to throw my bouquet and when that had been safely caught by Germaine, we threw a Frisbee. I was too happy perhaps to take it all in.

Towards the end of the afternoon I found myself upstairs in my bedroom, with Mama sitting on the bed beside me.

"Well, my dear," she said. "You've married a handsome young man."

I smoothed the satin dress over my knees and said nothing.

"I'm very pleased we know his family so well and it's such a good family."

"Yes," I said. I could hear the talking and laughter coming up from downstairs. There was a little silence between my mother and me, then she took my hand.

"You remember what I said to you when you first told Papape and me that you were going to marry Michel?"

"Of course."

"I don't want you to think that either of us disapprove of your choice. We're both so happy for you."

"He still makes you uneasy, doesn't he?"

"No. We love Michel, of course we do. But…well, yes, sometimes I *am* uneasy. Not your father, I think. Perhaps men understand one another better. But sometimes I have to wonder why Michel can never look me in the eye."

"He's shy, Mama."

"He is, but it's been three years now and I often wonder why someone so young would have something to hide."

"There's nothing."

She tipped her head down to look me in the face. "He's only twenty. Why does he act with me as though there *is* something?"

"I don't know." I could hear the voices downstairs of Oncle Louis Leo Patrice. Michel would never speak loudly enough to be heard above the chatter. I wondered if he was wondering where I was.

"There's something, something," Mama said. I thought she may have shaken her head slightly. "We may never know what it is but something's troubling him."

I said nothing and Mama made a small sigh.

"Perhaps it's better we don't know," she said.

"I'll look after him, Mama."

"There's no doubt about that, Denise." She had let my

hand go but now she took it again. "No doubt at all."

The two of us sat a minute without saying anything further. I was thinking about Michel, anxious to be at his side.

"I saw Dr. Boudreau Wednesday," Mama said abruptly.

"He's here," I said.

"I saw him at the hospital. We talked about Papape."

"What about Papape?"

"He's a Deveau, Denise."

"We're all Deveaus," I laughed. "Except you."

She didn't laugh with me.

"Dr. Boudreau said…he said if he was an insurance salesman, he wouldn't insure Papape's life for a nickel."

"What?"

"His heart."

"Papape's fine," I said. "He looks fine."

But a shadow crossed my mind again. Mama looked at me.

"He's a Deveau," she said. "And the Deveaus are cursed with bad hearts."

"Is Papape sick?" I was alarmed now but she shook her head. "We're all Deveaus, Mama," I repeated. "We can't all be sick."

"Of course not." She held my hand more firmly. "You're all my children too, all Bourgeois children too. A name isn't everything."

"No, it's not.

"But we must look after your father."

Downstairs, the little party continued. I saw Papape sitting down at one point but he caught my eye and smiled faintly. Then I saw Michel, just inside the kitchen.

He was having a beer and talking with Marie Anne, a young woman who lived in the hamlet of Plateau. She was laughing and he was nodding, but shyly, in his way. I saw him lean towards her and tell her something and I saw her smile, look down and say something back.

62

Concerning Oxygen

he chest pain and the pressure in my arms woke me about one o'clock. I rang the bell again.

"It's bad," I said. "I do need my nitro."

"No no." The plump nurse made a kind of dry laugh. "You just need more oxygen."

She turned the knob on the tank and went out without another word. I lay still and waited but the pain got worse. I rang again.

"Please," I said. "Please bring me my nitro pills."

"Look." She was standing at the end of the bed, far from me. "I'm sorry you're so worried and your nerves are so bad. But we've given you a sedative and, believe me, this pain isn't your heart. It's in your mind. You've got oxygen."

She turned to go and as she did, I saw my father. I didn't see him in the room of course, but his face suddenly and vividly appeared in my mind. He was smiling.

"Wait," I said. The nurse turned and looked at me. "My dad died young of a bad heart," I blurted. "Both my brothers got bad hearts. If any of them were here—if any middle-age man was here—would you treat him like this?"

She looked at me a moment but didn't say anything.

"I need help," I said.

"You're fine," she said.

She went out and I lay back on the pillow.

I saw Papape. He was sitting at the wheel of the Co-op delivery truck waiting uncomplainingly. I was just coming out of Bernadette's house in Belle Marche. I'd gone in with him to deliver the groceries that they ordered regularly. It was Saturday and this Saturday was my turn to help. Not that Papape needed help but those treasured days were his gifts to us, when or Ronald or Wilfred Normand got to proudly beside him his rounds and course slow him down considerably. The truck's big box was lined with shelves filled with canned goods and non-perishable food for cus-tomers who'd forgotten something when calling in an order. All the shelves were equipped with doors so nothing would fall on the floor when Papape was driving. Under the shelves was a little crate of assorted candies, bars, chips and gum that he sold for children. This was the Treasure Chest.

"What will you have today, Denise?" Papape asked.

"I want a Buried Treasure Bar."

"How about two?"

I looked up at his face in delight and saw him smiling. During that long night, I looked up at him again and again. I'd grown to understand my enemy, the pain, and knew I could face it with the nitro as my defence. Now there was no nitro and I was alone with my father to comfort me.

In the morning, Dr. Baillie came in looking tired. He asked me how I felt. I said not good. He ordered another EKG and the inverted Ts were still there. He sat down in the chair beside my bed.

"Denise, I'm not sure what's going on here. You're an unusual case. I'm going to ask Dr. Aucoin to book you into Victoria General Hospital in Halifax. They're equipped to investigate this further."

"That's good."

"Yes, it's good, but I'm afraid it may take some months."

I laughed. "I'll wait."

He sat thinking another minute with a sort of frown, then got up and crossed over to the tubes and oxygen equipment. He knelt and examined them, then went out and came back with a man who had some tools. Apparently there was a leak. The oxygen had been flowing out into the atmosphere, which hadn't really needed it as much as I needed it. Papape, I thought, you saw me through without nitro or oxygen.

Breathing and Writing

ou could be seductive, Cheticamp, stretched out on the shore as you are, inviting us all to take our time, raise our children and tend to our work in your slanting space between sea and hills. And in May, when the hard season was well passed, it seemed impossible to imagine a better place.

I looked up at the clock on my office wall. It was almost noon. Under the clock was the 1974 calendar with its picture of Aucoin's Bakery and the felt pen circles around appointment dates for Gilles' allergy test and the hair dresser. I was alone, as was normal for this time of year. Michel was fishing off Newfoundland.

My daughter Michelle was six that year and as I did every morning after breakfast, I'd put her on the bus to École NDA. Gilles was four. It was a warm spring and I could hear his voice—and those of Kevin and Troy and Danny and Dale—through the screen door, the meandering conversation of children at play, sometimes monotones—little mouths speaking whatever was passing through little heads—then abruptly strenuous or petulant or excited or bossy.

I looked back at my work. The month was drawing to a close—it was the twenty-third already—and I was drawing up the Texaco books for May. The phone rang.

"It's Papape," Mama's voice said. "His heart."

I sat with the phone in my hand, briefly unable to respond. From the receiver I could hear in the background the paging system outside her office door on the main floor of our Sacred Heart Hospital.

"He's alive," she said. "He drove himself here. He's unconscious now but he's alive."

So it had happened. We'd watched it approaching the way they say people caught on a trestle bridge watch the approach of a slow freight: suspended, almost puzzled. We'd watched the exhaustion grow worse, the blue color around his lips, the chest pain he tried so hard to hide, the endless spoonfuls of soda.

Mama spoke. "I'm afraid he's going to die. I've seen plenty of this. It's not good."

"I'll be there," I finally managed to say.

My brother Normand was twenty-seven, a year older than me. He was a teacher at École NDA and lived at home with Mama and Papape. He loved the outdoors as much as I did and he'd often go scuba diving with our new doctor, J. C. Aucoin. He was a quiet man, Normand, a man of gentle appearance, and the wide horn-rimmed glasses with their thick lenses made him seem more so. But he had this strange calm about him, so different from his sister.

The school secretary brought him to the phone. By then the

first shock had passed and I was frantic instead of paralyzed, confused about what I should do with my young son, who was still playing in the backyard, with my mother, my father.

"Take it easy," Normand said. His tone of his voice was even and slow. "I'll go to the hospital now for a few minutes, then I'll be over to pick up Gilles. I'll get Michelle from school and look after them while you go up to the hospital."

"But you have to teach."

"That's not important, Denise. Anyway, my class is seeing a dental hygienist this afternoon. No one will miss the teacher."

"Thank you, Normand. Thank you."

"We thought this might happen but we're not in it alone, are we?"

"No. Thank you."

Mama stood in the corridor, head down, seeming thin and frail and alone. I remembered Normand's words.

"I'm here, Mama," I said.

She looked up and I saw her expression tinged with desperation.

"He was at the Co-op getting ready for his afternoon deliveries. The pain came on so quick and he sat down. He thought it would get better but it got worse. Oncle Louis Leo happened to pass by and saw him." Mama's brother was the manager of the Co-op. "He saw Papape was in trouble and Papape told him it was like an elephant sitting on his chest and crushing him and Louis Leo said we've got to call the ambulance right away but he couldn't get Papape to agree."

I thought about how stubbornly we all cling to our

everyday lives even as the ground shifts under us.

"Papape got in his car and drove himself to the hospital," Mama was saying. "Can you imagine? Louis Leo followed him. They climbed the front steps of the hospital and came in the door. He collapsed on the floor in the lobby."

Dr. Aucoin was beside us. He had been our family doctor since Dr. Boudreau had retired. Mama held my arm tightly.

"Marie Louise," he said. "I've just seen Luby. He's regained consciousness and he's resting now."

Mama seemed to tap all her strength in that moment. There was no sign of tears.

"Can I see him?" she asked.

"I think we should let him rest a while."

She nodded. "Will he live?"

Dr. Aucoin didn't answer right away. He sort of studied her face. "I don't know," he said.

He did live, but the easy-going man I'd known all my life was gone. I'd only been in his room a few minutes and he was still asleep when an orderly came in, a sandy-haired, kind-faced, soft-spoken man of fifty. He had something on a tray. He gently woke my father.

"Luby? Dr. Aucoin has ordered a catheter for you. It will make it easier for you to pass water. You won't have to strain."

Papa's eyes snapped open and he fixed the orderly with a stare.

"You, you get out of here." He shot a look at the catheter. "And take that thing with you."

The orderly stepped back. "Luby, it'll help you."

"If I need to pee I'll let you know and if I don't happen to notice, I'll pee right here in this bed."

"Papa…" I began.

"Get out," he said to the orderly.

There was a lot of heart damage and he would remain in the hospital another three weeks. During that time I grew to know Dr. Claudie Aucoin better. Tall, good-looking, dark haired, with huge hands, in his role as Dr. Aucoin he was unusually professional in manner, always dressed in suit and tie, full of business, serious, though a good listener. This was the man at work. Then there was the Claudie I'd heard so much about, my brother Normand's sporting companion, roughly dressed and full of the devil, a man of many and changing hobbies: Ski-Dooing, camping with friends high in the mountains, cooking huge steaks, drinking beer, trout fishing and moose hunting in Newfoundland, scuba diving, motorcycling, speed boating, taking anybody up in his plane who had the guts to go with him. These contrasts instilled the greatest of respect in his Cheticamp patients. I was no exception, though I couldn't foresee the role he was to play. Normand was godfather to Claudie and Betty Ann's third child, Johanne Louise. He was "Claudie" to Normand, Papape and Mama—and to me, except when I was in his office, when he was somehow transformed into Dr. Aucoin.

Work was one of the pillars of my father's life. Now Dr. Aucoin told me that he would never work again.

"Your father will soon find out how little he'll be able to do," he said to me one afternoon a few days after the attack. "He's not to attempt any stairs for at least a month and when he does, he'll have to take each step very slowly."

"My mother says she's having a toilet installed in the

corner of their bedroom."

"He'll need it."

The next day a nurse went in to give my father his medication and found his bed empty. There was an anxious search throughout the hospital. They found him gasping for breath on the top floor.

"What are you doing here?" the nurse demanded.

Papape shrugged. "Wanted to find out how it felt, climbing stairs."

We may have had plenty of warning but that failed to protect us from being almost overwhelmed by my father's fate. The families of Cheticamp were often large and extended and we'd all witnessed the wearing away of the generations— grandparents, uncles and aunts. Perhaps we imagined we'd be able to face the loss of a parent with the same composure. I had my children and my love for Michel, but for Normand, who actually lived with our parents and who was by far the most soft-hearted of the four siblings, it was a daily struggle. He and I would go together to visit Papape in the hospital and afterwards, in the parking lot, for all his calm and cool, Normand would sometimes sit beside me at the wheel and weep like a child.

The day my father was discharged, the man came straight home, poured himself a big glass of Governor General rum topped up with water, sat back in his La-Z-Boy chair and lit up an Export A.

In the months that followed, he struggled to adapt to a life of enforced idleness and we struggled to adapt to a new father. I gradually returned my attention to my husband and children, though when Michel was at sea and Michelle at school, Gilles and I would go over and take Papape for a walk along a path that led through the woods. I'd watch his desperate shortness of breath and manage to persuade myself that these excursions were somehow good for him.

Back at their house, it was hard to miss the change in a family that had always been characterized by peace and cooperation. Mama had started smoking in her fifties and almost always had two packs open at the same time. Similarly, she seemed to have two ketchup bottles open in the fridge at the same time and usually had two newspapers—that day's and the previous day's—open at the same time. My father had generally reacted to these little behaviours by carefully putting all her cigarettes in one package and pouring the contents of one ketchup bottle into the other and gathering up and disposing of the old papers. He continued now to do this, but with visible impatience. Mama for her part had developed a tense vigilance, watching my father's every move, fearful that he would die the next moment. Papape saw her fear and that too irritated him.

He was not one to talk about his discomforts. During one of our walks, I asked him what he planned to do about his diet and cigarettes.

He stopped for a moment, breathing hard. "Nothing," he said. "I'll live as long as God wants me to and I'll die when he wants me to."

"Aren't you afraid of dying?"

"No I'm not," he said. He started along the path. "Death can't be worst than this."

I wasn't prepared to understand what he was saying.

Even such an affliction can't entirely erase decades of harmony. The almost-destroyed heart still beat in a living man. That man and his wife would still play cards with their best friends, Edith and Wilfred Boudreau. Oncle Daniel, Mama's brother, and his wife, Louise, lived just down the road and would visit them often. They'd listen to music together and talk about old times and laugh. My brother Wilfred, who was a microbiologist for the federal government in a lab in Shediac, N.B., came home constantly. My brother Ronald, who worked with the patients at the Chinese Hospital in Montreal, would fly into Sydney regularly. When Michel was home from sea we'd have my parents over for dinner and the two men—they had drinking and working in common—always got along well. And Normand—cool, calm Normand—still lived at home and, saddened as he was, remained a pillar to both his parents.

For all that, as that spring of 1974 wore into summer, I felt a sense of unease, a sense of being slightly off balance as I went about my work from day to day. For me Cheticamp, in memory at least, was suffused with the sun that streamed across the harbour from the open sea beyond the island, and now that sunlight, when I think back about it, seemed dimmed by the sort of mist that sometimes foretells rain and by events that, looking back, appear as omens. That was the summer of the drowned boy, of course. He was one of three ten-year-olds playing in a canoe in the harbour below my parents' house. The canoe capsized and only two of the children made it to shore. Normand saw the crowd and an ambulance and went down. Everyone was searching for the boy but couldn't find him. Normand came back up to the house and got his scuba gear and entered the water. By the time he found the little body, the crabs were already biting at it. Then Normand came back to the house and wept. "If

I'd gone down sooner," he kept saying, "maybe I could have saved him."

That evening I stood at the kitchen sink washing the dishes. I looked out the window towards the sea and found myself worrying about Michel, something I'd seldom done before.

Still, it was summer and Cheticamp people are country people and country people love the summer. From my window during the day I could watch the boats coming in and going out of the harbour. I could hear the splashing and voices of what seemed like every child in our neighbourhood. Alex and Lucille next door had a swimming pool and were so generous, it had become more a community pool than a family pool. Day after day I drove the mile to my parents' house with Michelle and Gilles to visit Mama and Papape, drink tea, smoke cigarettes, look out at the street and harbour and talk. Sometimes I missed the days when I had visited by foot, pushing the children in the carriage. They'd long outgrown their carriage now.

We were still with Mama and Papape late one August afternoon—Michel was fishing so there was no hurry to get home—when Normand arrived back from scuba diving. We could hear the clanking of his tanks as he stowed his gear in the basement and then he sauntered in, his T-shirt wet in places, his dark hair across his forehead, his glasses slightly askew, and plunked himself in an armchair.

"Don't get that chair wet," Papape said.

"No no," Normand reassured him. He was a good-natured kid and he laughed as he brushed the hair from his eyes. "I'm mostly dry."

"Were you out with Claudie?" Mama asked.

"Yep. Out at La Bloc by the park. Roger and Winston were with us."

"How's Winston? I saw his mother yesterday." Mama was ironing as she spoke.

"Winston? Fine. He's getting good, too."

Normand and Claudie Aucoin were closer than ever. Whatever mad adventure Claudie was up for, Normand was up for it too. He was even willing to go up in Claudie's plane. That summer, though, it was all about scuba diving.

"Can you see anything under there?" Papape asked.

"Yeah, it's not bad. We're not too deep."

"What do you see?"

"Fish and stones and stuff. We're looking for wrecks and lobsters."

We all sat there, maybe a little dozy in the later afternoon heat, except for Mama, who just ironed on.

"Funny thing," Normand took out a cigarette. "When we

got back on shore, Claudie said I'd used a lot more oxygen than Winston or Roger."

Mama looked up. "Why'd you do that?"

"I dunno. But Claudie said he'd like me to have one of those heart tests, just in case."

"You're probably smoking too much," Papape said.

Normand laughed. He had an easy laugh. "Right. Like I'm the only smoker." He shrugged and got up. "Anyway, I've got to get changed. We're going out tonight."

"Where you going?" Papape asked.

"We're playing poker at Winston's."

He went off to his room.

"What's scuba?" Gilles asked.

Mama's iron thumped away at the ironing board.

"It's probably nothing," she said, more to herself than me.

The following week, we were back at my parents' and I saw Mama gesture to me from the hall. Papape was working on a puzzle with the children while they were all three eating the strawberry Jell-O he'd made for them.

In my old bedroom, Mama sat down on the bed.

"Shut the door," she said.

I shut the door and stood with my back against it. Mama was going to tell me something awful, that was for sure. I didn't want it slipping by me and escaping out into the world.

"Normand went up to the hospital and had an EKG. Dr. Aucoin asked him to."

"I know. What *is* an EKG anyway?"

"It's a test of the heart. The heart gives off little electrical signals while it works and an EKG machine picks them up and traces them on paper."

I felt an awful sinking feeling.

"Has he heard anything?"

She shook her head but her mouth was set tightly.

"No. No, he hasn't. But I was afraid Claudie might not want to talk to him about it because they're such good friends. And..." She looked away a moment. "And I suppose Normand wouldn't tell me. You know Normand."

"Don't worry, Mama. Really. It's probably okay."

"No. No, it's not okay." She looked at me intently. "That doesn't mean we should worry. No use worrying about things you can't change. But you must never never tell anyone about this. Ever."

"Tell them what?"

"Promise me."

"Of course I promise."

"I've got access to all the medical records. I never look at anyone's chart unless I'm asked to. But this is my son."

"You saw the report on the machine?"

"Yes, but I had no idea what it meant. Doctors are trained to read these things."

"Maybe it meant nothing."

"I copied the report and took it to someone I know—a doctor in cardiology, not Dr. Aucoin. Never mind who. I scratched out Normand's name and age and showed it to him. He said..." She stopped here but now I understood. I waited. "He said this patient...was...in trouble."

Her thin body tensed as she struggled. I stepped towards her and laid a hand on one shoulder.

"I told him the patient...was my son." There was a long silence. "He said he was sorry."

Cheticamp, little town that had bestowed much happiness on me, now you began to steal it away, but by such slow degrees, I hardly noticed at first. That summer of 1974 wore into fall. Normand returned to his work as a teacher and never said a word about the EKG. Michelle moved on from kindergarten to grade one. Fall wore to winter.

Now it was borne in on me how illness was something more than an unexpected vacation, a chance to catch up on the housework, stock up on Kleenexes and collect a comforting bouquet of sympathy. There are illnesses that arrive uninvited and don't know when to leave. You have no choice but to deal with them as best you can. My father now had congestive heart failure. His feet, ankles, and lower legs swelled and his angina pain required us to fabricate a sort of home-made nitro patch. My mother and I measured nitro using a popsicle stick so it wouldn't touch our hands. We applied it to Papape's arm and covered it with a piece of plastic cling wrap.

There was no fishing in January and February. Michel worked at home every day on the seine nets, repairing them and making new ones as he'd learned to do at a training course in Pictou in 1966. He didn't work at this all day and I enjoyed having him home. By early afternoon he would usually drop in at the Legion, which was next door to our house. With time I came to accept that I'd often have supper alone with the children and leave his on the stove. My philosophy was that people who don't depend on others and don't expect anything of others can't end up feeling disappointed. Michel eventually established a pattern: he'd come in and eat and then rest on the couch before he'd go back to the Legion or to the tavern and come home drunk late at night. I'd already learned not to depend on him to pick things up from the store for supper because I might not see him until nine. I missed his company on long winter evenings but from another perspective, it wasn't all that important. When you love someone that much, you find it easy to accept their little weaknesses. The new fishing season would begin in April and when the days began to lengthen in March and the ice left the harbour, Michel and his men started back to work on the boat, cleaning, painting, overhauling the gear and the engine.

The fifth of March, 1975 was what you might expect— the sky a Cape Breton winter gray but the clear, bone-cold of January already well behind, as far behind as the first true April days of spring lay ahead. I got Michelle off to school and sat down in my office to review my client's books.

A few blocks away, my mother set off to Sacred Heart Hospital to begin her day as head of accounts. At noon she sat for lunch in the cafeteria, chatted with Gloria, a nurse she'd always liked. When she was done, she walked to the employee break room until lunch hour was over. She returned to her desk and began to work on a report to be typed by her secretary and sent to the Nova Scotia Department of Health. She wrote the report by hand and was almost through when she noticed she was having trouble writing the numeral *8*. It was something about the curves. She tried it again and again but the *8* wouldn't come out right. She took a scrap of paper and wrote the numerals *1* to *10*. This wasn't as easy as it should have been. She wrote her name. That wasn't easy either. She took her scrap of paper and walked down to the emergency department. Claudie Aucoin was there. He took her blood pressure: 160 over 100. Not good.

"Marie Louise, I'd like to admit you immediately."

Mama shook her head.

"No." She could be a stubborn woman. "No. I'm too busy, Claudie. I feel fine, really. It'll pass."

He must have looked at her very sceptically.

"It's extremely mild," she said.

"We've got to get that blood pressure down." He took out his prescription pad. "Take this down to the pharmacy."

She took the paper. "I think I might just go home and rest a bit," she said

"Yes. Please do that. But take the pills and tell Luby he's to call me if there's any change."

"I'll call you myself," Mama said.

About 2:30 Papape called me. As soon as I got there I noticed her mouth was slightly crooked. When she went into the kitchen to make tea, her right foot ever so slightly lagged.

"Of course, of course." She came back in, sat down, waved her hand gently from her chair as she lit a cigarette. "I've had a little stroke. We see these all the time. It happens when you get older."

"I'll call Dr. Aucoin."

"No, Denise. No, that's not necessary, dear. I've seen him already. I'll be okay after a good rest and now I've got the blood pressure pills. It's a wonder what these pills do for blood pressure."

"Okay, maybe. But let me drive you over to the hospital, just for the night. Just in case."

"Listen to Denise, Marie Louise," Papape wheezed from his La-Z-Boy. Mama shook her head.

"No, Denise. I spend all day in that hospital. I'm tired of it. In fact, I'm just plain tired. I'm going to bed."

Papape always got up early and made breakfast for Mama while she got herself ready for work. She came in and sat at the table.

"Marie Louise," Papape said. "Your mouth."

"What?" She slurred the word.

The Acadian Inn had changed owners and now went by a less dignified name: the Acadian Lounge. It was immediately across the road from my parents' house and men gathered there for morning coffee before going to work. Papape looked out the window. Dr. Aucoin's car was still in the parking lot.

"Marie Louise," he said. "Stay sitting at the table." He went down to the Inn and brought Claudie Aucoin back. Dr. Aucoin took one look at Mama.

"You're having trouble, Marie Louise?" he asked as soon as he walked into the kitchen.

"Yef," Mama said.

"I want you to come with me to the hospital, Marie Louise. Now."

I went to see her around 9:30 that morning. By then her right hand was partially paralyzed. She was sitting in bed but seemed strangely relaxed and at peace.

When I returned about 1:00 P.M. with Normand, Dr.

Aucoin told us she would be sent by ambulance to the Victoria General Hospital in Halifax, where she'd be under the care of a neurologist. The trip would take about four and a half hours. A nurse would accompany her but a member of the family had to go. I looked at Normand. I had a husband away at sea, two young children to look after, and a sick father who was worried to death. But from the look in Normand's eyes, I knew it would be me in the ambulance. The man was just too soft hearted to see his mother in this condition

"Please, Denise," he said. "I'll look after everybody at this end."

The ambulance wended its way down the coast and across mainland Nova Scotia to Halifax. I sat on the bench beside Mama and considered how my carefully constructed world was unravelling. I looked down at Mama and she'd occasionally look up at me and make a faint, crooked smile. What could she be thinking?

From the day of the stroke to the day she wrote her letter—the famous letter—was about eight months. Her right leg and right hand were partially paralyzed and her mouth was crooked, though she was able to talk with some difficulty. The neurologist and physiotherapist were emphatic that she must be left to learn to do everything for herself and the physiotherapy started immediately. It was almost too painful to watch her fierce devotion to these tiresome exercises.

The morning of her discharge, we had a final meeting with the neurologist. He reminded her that unless she told her mind to lift her right leg every step she took, she would drag her right foot for the rest of her life. Then he took a deep breath and explained to her that she would never be able to write again. Mama dropped her eyes. That was the end of her accounting work at Sacred Heart Hospital.

"There's something else," the neurologist said. "What's happened to you is nothing you could have controlled. It was an accident that could have happened to anyone. It's nothing to do with the few cigarettes you've been smoking recently or the kind of food you've been eating. Don't let anyone make you feel guilty in any way."

"It's nobody's fault," Mama repeated.

"That's right."

"But it's my job to fix it."

"That's right too."

On April first she came home. It was spring now—real spring, with the ice gone from the harbour and the fields beginning to green on the island beyond—and she set to work with an awesome determination. She exercised the muscles around her mouth by sticking her tongue out and twisting it in a variety of grimaces; within a short time, her mouth had straightened. She then concentrated on her walking, using weights on her right foot. She indeed had to consciously lift that foot for every step she took but never once did I see it drag. Her hand took longer. She started by squeezing a rubber ball, then she began lifting a one-pound weight, then a two-pound weight, then a five-pound weight. One afternoon she asked me to put three quarters on the table. Three days later she managed to pick up one quarter, but when she'd mastered the quarters, she went to work on dimes. Every day she tried to peel a potato, her mouth set in a tight line of concentration. The controls and movements we use to perform the simplest of tasks are so delicate, so intricate, when something disrupts even one component— the motor control of small muscles, for example—it reveals a whole world of mechanisms. Mama chipped at potatoes and chopped at potatoes and scraped at potatoes and one day in the summer of 1974 she peeled a whole potato. Perhaps that's why, as pitiful as it was to watch her scratching away with pen and paper, we never quite lost hope.

About a month after the stroke, there was a knock on my back door. Sister Kathleen was the administrator at Sacred Heart Hospital, where Mama had been in charge of accounting. I asked her in and shooed Gilles out to play. Sister Kathleen looked around.

"Charming old house," she said.

I chuckled at her politeness. "It has served us pretty well but we're going to renovate it completely."

"Really? I like the old houses of Cheticamp."

"Yes, but when you live in one you want it to suit you, not the other way around."

"I suppose." She looked serious. "I understand that your mother is recovering."

"She's a strong woman."

"I know that. We all know it. But the stroke has disabled her, of course, and I know she has some trouble with her speech."

"That's right. If she's under any stress."

"Right. Right." She nodded, looking at me.

"Sister Kathleen," I said. "If you're here to tell me that my mother no longer has a job, it's okay. We've got other things to worry about. My father's disabled from a heart attack and I'm afraid we've got our hands full. I hope everything will be okay at the hospital."

She nodded again. "They're not exactly okay, Denise. We have no one to do our accounting. Your mother was valuable to us and we're grateful to her."

I didn't say anything.

"We know you're running an accounting business from home."

"I have an office here."

"And we were wondering if we could interest you in doing the same at our hospital."

I stared at her.

"We thought your mother could accompany you when she's well enough and she could help you could learn the ropes."

"I'd…Thank you. I'd be interested but I'm sorry to tell you … someone should have told you…I have no degree in accounting. I taught myself and…" I was going to have a hard time saying this. "And I quit school at seventeen. I got my

Grade XII by going to night school."

"Fine, Denise. You could work on a temporary basis until we were comfortable with your handling of the job. Then, if everything's to everyone's satisfaction, you could become a permanent member of the hospital staff. Your personal and professional reputation is excellent. I'm not sure we'd gain much by hiring someone just out of school. Diploma's aren't everything."

"I believe that myself."

"It's only common sense."

I gave her a good long look and she looked right back.
November. I was visiting Mama one afternoon. At some point she sat down at the table and took out a single sheet of paper and set it in front of her. She picked up her pen. With great deliberation, she wrote a note and signed her name. She took out an envelope and addressed it. When she'd finished, she looked exhausted but there was also something fierce in her expression.

"Could you take this to the post office, Denise?" she asked. "It's a thing I wanted to tell someone."

When I was safely down the driveway, I looked at the envelope. It was addressed to her neurologist in Halifax, the one who'd assured her she'd never write again.

A Hard Case

ormand married Helen Merry in 1978. He was thirty-one that year—rather an advanced age for a groom in Cheticamp—and Helen Merry had two children of her own, teenagers Shunda and Ian, but Normand was a person guided by his own slightly eccentric star. He loved kids even though he worked with them every day and for him, Helen Merry's children were just two new friends. Shunda even stood at the wedding for her mother. Claudie Aucoin stood for Normand.

Normand and Helen had a nice bungalow built where you could see the boats coming in and going out and the family seemed happy. Things had changed, of course. Normand did less charging around with Claudie—planes and bikes and speedboats and Ski-Doos and trout fishing trips to Newfoundland and scuba diving in the waters near the National Park—there was less of all that. At the time, I thought he was settling down to a comfortable middle age. There was more golfing, for example.

Things were changing too for my parents. Normand had been so good to them—a constant presence in a house occupied by two people closely brushed by death—they had to miss him even though we all tried to fill the void left when he moved out. I visited them almost every day. "We're both fine," Papape would say. "We've adjusted fine. Quit fretting." I still worried, useless though it was. They were old and unwell. Wouldn't they be lonely, even if they weren't alone?

90 The year after the wedding, Normand woke up one morning to discover that his left foot and lower leg had turned dark purple. He went up to the hospital and Claudie Aucoin arranged that he go immediately by ambulance to City Hospital in Sydney. I saw him briefly and was horrified. I'd never seen a foot that color. Normand remained calm.

"Aren't you scared?" I asked him.

"Denise, don't worry." He shifted his foot slowly. It must have been extremely uncomfortable. "Whatever happens, I'll be okay."

Helen and I drove to Sydney. By the time we arrived at the emergency, they'd already done the arteriogram. Normand greeted us with a smile.

"It's official," he said. "I've got severe peripheral vascular disease—atherosclerosis."

We must have looked puzzled.

"That's hardening of the arteries to you. They're going to operate in the morning."

I went to sit down but there was no chair. Helen looked stricken.

"What will they do?" she asked him.

Normand helped himself to the water on his bedside table. He shrugged. "They're going to replace my aorta and my iliac and my femoral arteries with some sort of grafts. Simple as that."

The beds were full and he spent all that day and all that night on a stretcher. Helen and I could do nothing but walk around, go out for smokes and worry one another about whether they could save his leg. The next morning we lingered at the motel. I tried to read but couldn't concentrate. Finally, when I could take it no longer, we drove to the hospital.

He was sleeping. He wasn't a big man but he looked so small in that bed, I felt a kind of horror. Eventually he began to wake and finally he looked up at us.

"I told you there was no reason to worry. I'm still here."

"The operation was a success." I couldn't think what else to say.

"Yeah." He made a weak smile. "I've got plastic arteries now." He seemed to doze a bit but opened his eyes again. "Better than nothing."

A month later he went back to teaching and maybe four months had passed when he came to visit me one night after supper. He'd often drop in but this wasn't one of his regular visits.

"I just want to make a phone call," he said. "Is that okay?"

I looked at him. "Of course. Is everything alright?"

"It's the best." He was already dialling. "I just don't want Helen to find out about it. Or anyone else. Hello? Hello, Dr. Naqvi? It's Normand Deveau. I'm sorry to call you at home."

I knew Naqvi had been his surgeon. Normand was telling him that he was okay but he had pain in his leg when he was walking and he could only walk short distances. There was a long silence while he listened to whatever Naqvi was saying, only responding "Right, right" every now and again.

When he hung up he looked a bit sheepish.

"Well?"

"It's fine," he said.

I just raised my eyebrows and after a moment of indecision, Normand nodded.

"It's fine. Dr. Naqvi did the best he could with what he had to work with. My arteries were in really bad condition, right? He said I was lucky to be alive. We knew that anyway. He knows it hurts to walk but he said that when he had me on the table, he decided that I'd probably prefer a painful leg to no leg at all." He took a deep breath and then smiled. "That's it, then. It's all fine."

So now he knew his fate. He never complained then or later. He seems not to have discussed it with Mama and Mama did not discuss it with Papape because she felt Papape had enough to cope with. She talked to me about it only because she had to tell someone.

Normand couldn't race or dive or skidoo any more but he bought a cart and kept at his golf. After a big rain, his would be the only cart allowed on the course. Cheticamp is such a little place, every second person Normand saw in the run of a day would ask him how he was. "The best," he'd always say. "The best."

In June of the next year, 1980, Mama and Papape sold the family home and moved into a retirement residence where they were surrounded by friends. I wasn't sorry. The young couple who bought the house were just starting their life together and they loved the place and the view of the sea.

When we were kids Mama had planted rose bushes that had somehow survived through the years and each summer the young woman would visit her and bring her one of those roses.

The next year Normand was back in Sydney to undergo surgery again. Michel and I and our son Gilles flew into Sydney on our way back from St. Pierre and Miquelon, where Gilles had been in a hockey tournament. I was exhausted— I often was then—but of course we visited Normand in the hospital. He was hooked up to an IV and a tube in him was draining brownish liquid into a bag by the floor. He gave us a wave when we walked in and then sent me to a corner store for cigarettes because they wouldn't let him smoke in the room and he was too weak to get to the smoking room.

"Where're you going to hide them?"

"My feet." He gave his little laugh. "My feet are real cold. I told the nurse I had to have some socks."

I put a cigarette and a pack of penny matches in one of his socks. He hobbled off to the bathroom, which was close by. When he was done, I helped him get settled back in bed. He seemed cheerful, unworried. Michel was sitting in a chair in the corner. He'd already stopped in at a few bars by then.

"This isn't good, Normand," he said. "Aren't you worried? I mean, Papape had a heart attack and you're his son."

Normand smiled. "What do you mean? I'm so young and I'm already living on borrowed time?"

"Yeah. Something like that."

Normand shrugged. "Whatever happens, happens." He raised his eyebrows. "Right, Michel? Worry just makes more pain, right?"

"I suppose," Michel said.

We said goodbye about six and by the time we left Sydney Michel was feeling no pain of any sort. I drove the two hours to Cheticamp.

94

A Going Off
A Coming Back

By 1982 Cheticamp had a popular fish market on the main street close to where we lived. Perhaps that wasn't surprising for a village that lived by fishing. It was a tiny, busy place that sold the best take-out fish and chips ever. That oddly cool July day I'd gone down to the market and picked out a big piece of fresh salmon caught that morning. There are a lot of ways to cook salmon but I had a favourite recipe. I lightly browned butter in the pot, then chopped onions and added them along with the salmon pieces. Salt and pepper and a little bit of water were the only other ingredients. I let the whole thing simmer very slowly with the cover on. It sounds simple, I know, but when you have fish that fresh, the whole idea is to allow the flavour to come through.

The children would be home for supper. Gilles and the other boys were on their bikes in the woods. Michelle and her best friend, Angela Aucoin, were driving the three-wheeler in the big field way up behind the house. School had only been out a week or so.

The phone rang. Carol Dugas was a nurse on duty at the Cheticamp hospital.

"Denise, we've admitted your father."

My hand groped for the stove controls almost like it had a mind of its own, as though it knew I was going to be busy now. "Is he alive?"

"Yes, he's alive."

"I'll be right over."

"Look, Denise, don't rush. He's stable."

"How stable?

"Stable. But Denise, I'm pretty sure this is his last admission."

"I understand."

I turned everything off. It was cooked anyway. I looked at the clock: it was almost six. I scribbled a note for the children and left it on the table. I found the car keys in the dining room after a distracted search and stopped in front of the mirror to pat my hair in place. The kitchen door opened and Michel came in.

"Papape's back in the hospital," I said. I snatched my purse from the counter. "Dinner's on the stove."

Michel nodded, drew a cigarette from his package. "When'd he go in?"

"Just an hour or so, I guess."

"Okay. You'll take the car?"

"Yes."

He sat down. He didn't seem to have been drinking.

"You mind if I go down to Yarmouth with Edgar Leblanc? He's having that new boat built and he wants to check it out."

"Of course I don't mind. How long will you be gone?"

"I don't know. A couple of days at the most."

"Fine. That's fine. When will you leave?"

"About twenty minutes or so. I'll call you from there."

"Sure, Michel. Sure, that's fine."*

He was conscious but his breathing was severely laboured. Papape looked up at Normand and Mama and me and smiled. There was a brief, awkward silence.

"You sure picked a warm day," Normand said. Papape smiled again. I cut across this approach immediately.

"Papape." I sat beside Mama, who was seated near the head of the bed. "Papape, you know you might not be coming out of it this time, right?"

He looked at me steadily and nodded.

"You know how much we all love you, don't you?"

He nodded again and I could see the tears in his eyes. I glanced over at Mama and Normand and I saw how they seemed frozen in their positions. I looked back at Papape.

"Are you afraid of dying, Papape?"

"No," he said. His voice was quite clear. "You know I'm not. Don't worry about me. I'll be fine."

I reached across and hugged him and then Mama hugged him.

"I love you, Luby," she said. "I love you so much."

Out of the corner of my eye I saw Normand weeping out of sight by the door. He seemed to take his own life lightly enough but when it came to other people, he was still the softy.

Papape's sister, Tante Marie, stayed in the room through

the night while the rest of us got some sleep. The next morning Wilfred and Marie France arrived and they and Normand and Mama and I met Father Tremblay on the steps of the hospital as he was leaving.

"He's sleeping now," Father Tremblay said, "and breathing heavily."

In French we call it *le ralle de la mort,* that breathing. It's how a person who was once big and capable surrenders his remaining strength: rhythmically and noisily. It had begun already but Wilfred had a hard time accepting that he had missed this last chance to speak with his father.

"Papape," he said over and over. "Papape. Can you hear me? Squeeze my hand if you can hear me."

Our vigil ended the next day. Michel came back that evening. My youngest brother Ronald flew into Sydney Airport with Papape's sister, Tante Martine. Oncle Claudius and Tante Jeanne picked them up at the airport.

Twice a year Papape had made a big pigs' feet dinner. He'd simmer those trotters slowly the whole day and in the evening Claudie Aucoin and all Normand's friends would crowd in at my parents' table and gorge themselves on the treat. There was a lot of laughing. Now these same men were the cook's pallbearers at the Église St. Pierre in Cheticamp. The next morning Michel left for the fishing grounds off Newfoundland.*

April 28, 1983. The ice was off the harbour. I'd worked most of the afternoon at my desk in the office at home, chewing on Tums for the indigestion that had started to nag me almost every day, getting up now and then to stretch my legs, looking out the window at the expanse of blue water and the still-brown fields on the island beyond. By evening, when the kids had finished their homework and gone to bed, I could finally put my feet up and turn on the TV. Michel was probably out at the Legion. The phone rang.

Marie France's voice was trembling.

"Denise?"

In that moment I felt an awful foreboding.

"Denise, Wilfred's had a heart attack."

Wilfred was the toughest, most self-assertive of my brothers. He'd graduated from university and immediately landed a job with the federal government, working in a lab in Shediac, New Brunswick. In 1968 he'd married Marie-France Degrace, the youngest of nine children in a Shippigan, New Brunswick family, and they were raising their three children in Shediac. I saw a lot of Wilfred and his family during their frequent returns to Cheticamp and I'd grown exceptionally close to Marie France. I saw how she stood up to Wilfred—she didn't have much choice—but the arguments, or maybe the truthfulness that underlay those arguments, seemed to draw them closer together over the years. I couldn't help but notice how different this was from my marriage to Michel. We almost never argued.

Now Wilfred was in the hospital in Moncton, fighting for his life. I hung up the phone and saw my hands were shaking. I called Normand.

"That's three of us," he said, when he was sitting in my living room ten minutes later.

"This is the curse of the Deveaus," I said.

Normand shrugged. "Whatever it is, it's what we've got to

work with. At least *you're* okay."

"Me? Sure I'm okay. I'm a woman. It doesn't happen to women. But what about Ronald? He's just a kid." I started to cry. "I don't understand. Look at Wilfred. Look how trim he is. My God, he only eats what you need to stay alive and it's all healthy stuff. We're all outdoors people. What's going on? What about all the big fat guys? Why aren't they all having heart attacks?"

"There there," said Normand.

Wilfred survived, the left side of his heart badly damaged. The cardiologists were baffled. Heredity, they concluded. A mistake, a mistake in the genetic code. Normand and I talked about that almost every night. We have to pay for our mistakes. Our heredity was killing our men.*

"The cod are getting smaller and we're catching way less," Michel told me one morning when I was off work. "You know what's going to happen, don't you?"

I'd heard him come in about three the night before and now he sat at the kitchen table with a beer and cigarette.

"You know what's going to happen. The government's going to put a stop to cod fishing. That's what's going to happen. They're going to try to save what's left of the cod. Anybody left in the game is going to be out in the cold."

"What will you do?"

"I've already done it. Leo Boudreau—you know him, the lobster fisherman—he's going to be retiring. He needs help now so I'll work the traps with him for a couple of years, then buy his gear."

A few weeks later, he gave his resignation notice to his boat captain.

So, as I came to accept the sadness of my father's passing, and Normand's illness, and Wilfred's, I also rejoiced as a new life opened up for me. I would no longer be married to a man who was away for weeks on the fishing banks. Instead, I would have a husband who would be home in our own village every day. Yes, he drank too much. Yes, he didn't help a lot around the house—he couldn't even be trusted to go to the store for a quart of milk without disappearing for six or eight hours—but he *was* a good provider to me and the children and he *was* fun to do things with and of course he was as handsome as ever. If I was a contented woman before, I was truly happy now.

The Secret Retold

hich Cheticamp is the Cheticamp I remember? Or is Cheticamp a sort of recipe, something I use to cook together the memories? The village of my childhood is the predominant flavour—no doubt about that—but by the mid-eighties we Cheticantins had worked our variations and had almost covered the old flavours with new, spicier ones.

My children were growing. Gilles had his first Honda 50 motorbike when he was eight and a Kawasaki 80 when he was eleven. By the mid-eighties he and Michelle were experienced drivers of Ski-Doos in the winter and three-wheelers in the summer. When they were inside they played Atari games and sampled the electronic wonders of the new age. There was no talk of matching marbles or keeping hoola hoops from falling off hips, no traces of hopscotch chalk on the sidewalks. Meanwhile we the grownups were busy filling the grassy fields with a new arena, a new golf course, a new motel. The Acadian Inn, where I'd first heard English spoken, persisted a few years more as the Acadian Lounge, then burned to the ground one night and everyone stood and watched. So the past passed. New schools, new stores, new boats took its place.

Now in the spring of 1986 Gilles turned sixteen and his Oncle Raymond—Michel's sister's husband who owned Ray's General Store just across the street from us, offered him a summer job refilling shelves. Michelle was already working there at the cash register when she wasn't at school. After the second night, Gilles came home and sat himself in the hallway to the kitchen, on the bottom step of the stairs.

"Mama," he said. "We have to talk."

I stopped in the doorway and saw his grave expression.

"I hate my job. I'm not going back unless you force me to go. I'd rather do anything but fill up shelves."

I looked at him, sitting there, so distressed. "I hate it," he said.

"Okay, Gilles." I didn't want to protest too much. He was clearly seeking my permission. "But you'll have to talk to Oncle Raymond yourself. That's the right thing to do."

"I will. I promise, Mama."

"And you'll have to find yourself a job for the summer vacation. That's going to be here pretty soon."

He looked up and smiled. "Don't worry," he said. "I will."

I looked at him and realized how quickly he was growing into manhood. This is what I wanted, of course, but part of me didn't want to see my boy disappear into the man.

"Come on," I said. "Let's sit in the kitchen. I've made some brownies."

We were at the kitchen table when Michelle came in from visiting her friend Angela. She opened the fridge.

"We're having brownies," I said.

"I dunno," she said. "Maybe." I saw Gilles' eyes dart to Michelle once or twice while he was on his second piece.

"Mama," Gilles said suddenly. "You make pretty good money, right? At your job." Again, he glanced at Michelle, who sat down now and began to peel an orange.

"Yeah, I do. You know that."

"I mean, we could all get by on that, right? And Michelle and I will both have jobs in the summer, maybe winter too."

"What do you mean 'get by', Gilles?"

"You know what I mean, Mama. Papape. We don't need him financially."

I must have sat a moment without speaking.

"Mama, when is he ever here for us? We can't depend on him."

"I know there are problems, Gilles."

"Mama." Michelle looked up from her orange. "He's always drunk."

"I know it's a problem," I said. "But he's your father."

"He is." Gilles tried to catch my eyes with his but I found this a hard topic. "But just explain to us why we're still living with him. Please."

I realized I was embarrassed more than anything else.

"If we separated from your father, that would be the end of my marriage."

"Right."

"I love him too much to give him away to another woman."

They both nodded, very respectful, but kept looking at me.

"It's love, then," Michelle finally said.

"That's what it is."

Work filled all our lives that summer. I was now over ten years into my job as director of finance at Sacred Heart Hospital in Cheticamp. As a manager, I stood next in rank to the hospital administrator and when the administrator was on vacation or away from her post, I was acting administrator in charge of the entire hospital. Working with figures was my passion and from the very beginning, I loved my job. The first day I went to work Mama had said to me, "Denise, I'll give you one piece of advice, which I hope you'll never forget. To succeed at this job you have to be able to leave your work when your working day is over. Never bring your family problems to work, learn to concentrate strictly on your work when you're there and give your full attention to your husband and family when you're home."

As time went on, I took charge of the yearly budget and the monthly financial reports to the government, attended the monthly management meetings and monthly meetings with administrators and accountants from the whole Cape Breton area. I attended countless seminars to keep up with changes in the administration of Nova Scotia health care. These meetings were held at a different hospital each month and all attendees had to travel, mostly in the Sydney and Halifax area. I often checked in at a motel and returned home the following day.

I admit I loved dressing up in nice business clothes but the biggest extra was the bonds I eventually formed with many of the staff. At first I had the help of the angelic Sister Marie Louise Chiasson, and when she retired my friend and second cousin, Marthe Lefort—smart as a whip—replaced her. I was tireless and we ran a careful and efficient department.

Michel was lobster fishing now. He was as good a lobsterman as he'd been a cod fisherman. During the winter he would check each trap and make his repairs in preparation for the spring season.

That spring of 1986, a tiny flaw appeared. I worked fulltime, had two teenagers and a husband who until two years before had been away at sea most of the time except in the winter. I led a busy life but so did a lot of other women I knew. The flaw was that I noticed I was tired after work—much more tired than I remembered being. During breaks I asked my co-workers what they'd done the night before. They were all too happy to talk about it. Marie Eveline had scrubbed the ceiling and walls of one room. Jeanette had made eight meat pies. Marjolaine had cleaned all the ceiling light fixtures in her house. I said nothing.

Those evenings—when the world was coming alive again and everything had new energy—maybe those were the worst. Michel and the children were in the living room, talking, laughing, watching TV. I would be preparing supper, setting the table, mashing the potatoes and turnips, making gravy for the steak. More than once I stood at the stove with tears were running down my face, I was so tired. I would leave everything where it was, go to the washroom, take a few deep breaths, splash cold water on my face. No one noticed.

The tiredness became exhaustion and I struggled to hide it. I attended a meeting in Halifax. I checked in at a motel that night and after the next morning's meeting the others wanted to walk to a nearby restaurant for lunch. The walk and the fresh air will do us all good, they said.

"Come on, Denise!"

"No no. I just want to relax and think a bit."

I ate the apple and chocolate bar I had in my purse.

I didn't get much physical exercise at work and I knew I should, so I'd been going for a walk almost every day. This was becoming more and more difficult as the pain in my upper legs increased. I tried stopping until the pain went away but as soon as I started walking again, it came back. I tried walking backwards, which seemed easier for a while. At night there was a painful pressure in my upper legs but it would be gone by morning and I didn't have time to dwell on it. I couldn't ignore my arms, though. When I tried spring cleaning—the drapes and the ceiling globes—my arms became too painful and weak to continue. Then, as spring progressed, I started experiencing chest pain. I crunched Tums by the carload and hoped they'd start working for me soon. It was turning into a private hell, this trying to act normal.

Of course I was worried about my heart. I didn't want to sound a fool to Normand, who had real problems, but I asked him casually which part of his legs hurt. His lower back legs, he said—his calves—then he just woke one morning with a purple foot. Wilfred claimed he had no warning at all—felt fine until the day of his heart attack. These stories sounded nothing like me; they were cut and dry cases. I had to face the fact that I just might be crazy—and if not crazy, then overdoing it. Stressed. Overworked. Getting older. I had kids who were almost grown. Gilles had announced he would be fishing cod with Captain Yvon Boudreau that summer. Both he and Michelle had done exceptionally well at school that term. It was time to stop worrying about health fears and get on with looking after my family—my children, my hard-working husband, my aging mother and all my loved ones.

And so I arrived at that June day, Sneaker Day, with ten or twelve of us squeezed into two cars. Marthe Lefort, Gloria Leblanc, Marie Sophie Shomphe, Heather Leblanc were in our car—they were good friends then but much better friends later— and Germaine Campbell was driving. She turned off the main high- way and went up Cemetery Road. We were laughing and gabbing like schoolgirls who'd managed to sneak away at recess for a smoke. Actually a couple of us *were* smoking, our cigarettes held outside the car window in the warm breeze. *There* was pleasure: a beautiful day, good old friends, a cigarette, and all that during working hours. Somebody—I can't remem-ber who—started talking about Pauline Q. who'd been seen with Jacques Leblanc at a bar in Margaree Harbour just the week before. Jacques was married to Jeanne, a nice woman who worked at Marie's Salon. We all knew about it but that didn't stop us talking and saying how bad we felt for Jeanne, even though we didn't really know her, and how we all pretty much knew how it would end when she married Jacques,

who had a reputation for chasing women like Pauline Q.

"Somebody ought to tell her," Marthe said.

"Somebody ought to tell Pauline's husband," Gloria said.

"He already knows, I bet," Germaine said.

Nobody would tell anybody.

Up on the Plateau, we burst out of the cars. For some reason, even now, I can remember that sun on my face and those sounds that you didn't hear all winter and now they were all around you. Some of the women in the first car had actually started running and were way up the road, which was pretty flat for a stretch. The rest of us walked along, still talking, laughing. After a while, I personally had to stop laughing and after a bit I didn't talk too much but just concentrated on keeping up and even that got harder. The road turned up here, away from the village and the sea and towards the higher slope. The last of our group was way ahead of me now and my steps were getting short and slow. I think it was Gloria who realized I wasn't with them and she turned around.

"Denise!" she called. "Denise, come on! Come on!"

I stopped and smiled.

"Something wrong with your sneakers?" Marthe called.

I waved. "No." I couldn't call too loud. "No. You go on. I'm going back to the car. You go on."

Below us, the village of Cheticamp lay quietly in the midday sunlight. Beyond the village, the harbour and the island, beyond that the sea and its men at work in boats. A perfect day.

The Scribbled Heart

he nurse led the way and I couldn't help shooting a glance or two into the rooms that lined the long corridor. The Victoria General Hospital in Halifax was far bigger than the City Hospital in Sydney or my own Sacred Heart in Cheticamp. In every bed in every room of the cardiac wing lay a man, an older man, sixty at least. A few of them looked at me blankly as we passed. It was as though I'd stumbled into some sort of retirement club—the heart club—but I hadn't paid my membership dues and didn't belong.

When we reached my room, the nurse bustled around, opened the curtains, checked her papers.

"So your doctor's explained to you that you're here for an angiogram."

"Yes, I know. I know how it is. I'm sorry I don't speak English so well."

"That's fine, that's fine. So your angiogram is this afternoon and the doctors will thread a very fine tube called a catheter from your leg up to your heart and put some dye in your blood and take some x-rays that will show them what's going on."

"I understand. Does it hurt much? It's okay but I just want to know."

"No. It won't hurt. You'll be a bit sedated. You'll be fine. Who's here with you?"

"My husband drove me up." It was in the latter part of December and Michel was not out on the lobster boat. He would be spending the night with his brother and we would be driving back home the following day.

"Will they do an angioplasty if they find an occlusion in a coronary artery? I was just wondering."

She regarded me a long moment.

"They'll decide when they see the x-rays," she said.

I'd had months now to read about my disease and I knew the little balloon they called an angioplasty could make a big difference in some patients. I wanted to understand whatever I could. If I'd learned anything from my ordeal that night in Sydney, it was that you couldn't know too much and you couldn't totally trust anyone to know their job. My doctor had ordered me to lose twenty pounds before the angiogram and my dietician told me to do it by living off salads. But I was young and I couldn't face the idea that I might die eating salads. I decided instead to make steak and fries and maple ice cream part of my diet because they were among the things that sustained my spirit. I simply ate half my normal amount and told the dietician I was stuffing myself with lettuce and cucumbers. I lost the twenty pounds. It would help doctors to remember that patients can only take so much. I was stuck with a disease I wasn't ready for and every night I still went to bed thinking I'd be better in the morning. In fact I've always thought everything would be better the next morning.

The door opened and a tall, narrow-faced woman of forty

entered. I was struck immediately by her jet black hair and sharp blue eyes. She had a stethoscope around her neck and a white coat, so there was no doubt she was a cardiologist. She didn't smile but stood looking at me a moment, a little bit like the nurse had. She introduced herself as Dr. O'Hara.

"What are you doing here?" she asked.

I didn't like her tone.

"I'm surely not on no vacation," I said.

"I hope not." She looked at my chart. "Because we're very busy in this department."

I could feel her anger.

"I'm here because Dr. Aucoin and Dr. Baillie recommended I come here to have my heart checked out." I was struggling a bit. "Because inverted Ts showed up on my EKG and...

"I'll tell you right now," she interrupted. "We've got precious little time to waste on young women who think they know medicine and imagine they're sick."

"I..." But I couldn't think what to say next.

"Open your gown, please," she said, holding her stethoscope and bouncing it lightly in her hand.

When she was gone I looked over at my clothes and purse that were still on the chair. I felt an awful temptation to just get up and walk out, as I had at Cheticamp. There was nothing to stop me except that this was my only chance to find out what was really wrong and maybe get it fixed.

I was back in my room by three and lay there waiting and hoping. I knew an angioplasty could open a blocked artery and allow my heart the blood it needed to work right. That's all I needed: a little wider gap in a little tube.

The door opened and the narrow-faced doctor re-appeared holding a small sheet of blue paper. She sat in the chair beside the bed and drew a heart—my heart, for sure—and the major coronary arteries. It wasn't that bad a drawing. Then she scribbled out part of my right coronary artery and then she scribbled out one side of my heart. She turned the paper so I could see it better.

"So what does that mean?" I asked.

"It means you've got a blockage here, in your right coronary artery and a certain heart muscle, here on the right, is dead as a result."

I nodded.

"You've got angina."

"I know," I said. "So now what?"

"So that's what's wrong with you."

"So what will you do?"

"Do?" She looked annoyed. "We won't do anything. You're not a critical case and you can live with it. You'll be treated with medication. We've got a lot of really sick people in this department."

"You won't be doing anything at all?"

"I'll be sending you home."

When she'd gone, I noticed she'd left her little drawing on the blue paper and the scribbled out bit of heart. I was still looking at it when the head nurse came in to check my vital signs. I looked up at her, painfully self-conscious about my English.

"Excuse me, but have you got some doctor—a cardiologist? Another one?"

"You've just seen the cardiologist, haven't you?"

"I'd like to speak to another one about…some things."

She looked at me and not unkindly.

"I'll see what I can do," she said.

The man who came in was older than the woman cardiologist and had nothing of her manner. I can't recall his name but he listened carefully to my plea for help.

"I understand," he said finally. "I perhaps shouldn't say this, but there was a general consensus among the department cardiologists that we should perform an angioplasty. However, Dr. O'Hara was firm that it's unnecessary in your case and she's senior here. She's ordered an increase in your heart medications."

"So I just go home."

"I have to advise you personally to take it very easy. Don't exert yourself if you can help it."

"I've got a job and two kids."

"Right."

It's difficult to say what determines the connection between a doctor and a patient. I was to meet three other persons who had this Dr. O'Hara as their cardiologist and they adored her. They had, to be sure, twenty years on me. Perhaps she felt they'd earned her attention by growing older.

Michel and I left for Cheticamp the next morning, driving north to Truro and then east towards Cape

Breton. It was two weeks before Christmas, 1986, and this was a season I'd always loved. Now was when the Cheticamp harbour would freeze as smooth and polished as a mirror and I'd been proud to lace on a pair of my brothers' skates and whirl out onto the teeming ice. After I was twelve, I'd lace on my own pair of white skates, the proudest possessions of my childhood. At night we'd drag trees and branches to the middle of the harbour and build a bonfire that would light up that whole corner of the village. We'd lie on our backs in the snow and inhale the cold air and wiggle our frozen toes and look up at the hard twinkle of the stars.

The sky was gray ahead of me now on the highway and there were a few lonely flurries in the air. I sat silently beside Michel, who was driving. I'd been sent home to die, I thought, by a woman who irrationally resented my age and gender. Who gave her such power?

We crossed over the Canso Causeway that links mainland Nova Scotia to Cape Breton. The sky began to clear a bit and the sun peeked through and typically I began to cheer up. I'd always been taught our fate was in the hands of God, not other people, not some doctor in the Halifax Victoria General who, now I considered it more closely, had nothing to do with my fate.

I'd thought a great deal about the past in the months since my troubles began. I resolved from now on to move forward. I'd accept my illness and whatever it would bring. What else was there to fear? I'd heard the worst. Tomorrow would be better.

Work Left Undone

looked at the alarm clock, which was set for six. It was five-fifty-three. Something had awakened me.

It was March of 1987. Another spring was waiting to rouse a sleeping Cheticamp from another winter. The repair of nets and engines and gear was almost done. The ice in the harbour was growing soft.

I lay still a moment. Chest pain. The old familiar. I kept my nitro pills on my night table and I put two of them under my tongue. It would all be fine in a few minutes.

The alarm went off. The pain was worse now and spreading to my jaw and down both arms. Two more nitros, but the pain in my arms grew so bad, it overwhelmed the chest and jaw pain. My arms felt like they were going to burst, as though they were balloons blown so big they might blow up. I woke Michel up.

"Something's happening," I said.

Sacred Heart was only a few minutes away. Two attendants hurried me into the ER.

"My arms are going to burst!" I told anyone around me. The doctors pumped dose after dose of morphine through an IV. The chest and jaw pain subsided almost immediately but the pain in my arms backed off only slowly and reluctantly. For a long time—I don't know how long—I lay perfectly still, immersed in relief. The young doctor on duty came in again.

"I'm okay," I told him. "I'm okay. I'll go home now. I'm okay."

She looked at me. It was an odd expression—something between amusement and anger.

"Mrs. Poirier," she said. She made a little, humourless laugh. "You've just survived a subendiocardial infarct. That's a type of heart attack. Since you haven't gone to heaven, you're going to the ICU. An RN will watch over you. If your luck holds and you survive the night, we'll transfer you to Halifax first thing in the morning." She raised her eyebrows in an exaggerated expression, like you might have asked a naughty child a question. "Okay?"

"Okay."

I had no control over the situation. The staff were doing what they could. I gave up, relaxed, felt totally at peace. I was in God's hands so I was in good hands.

The next morning, I woke up to no pain but found Claudie Aucoin sitting by my bed.

"I got one last favour to ask you," I said.

"What do you mean, a last favour?"

"I mean, in case I don't make it back from Halifax."

"You're going to make it, Denise."

"Yeah, I know. But I want to ask you anyway if I can have a cigarette?"

He looked around. "Now?"

"One just like the one you're going to smoke with me," I said.

He took a cigarette from his pack and put it in my mouth, lit it. I knew he was a soft-hearted devil. It was the most important cigarette of my life.

An ambulance rushed me through Cape Breton that morning and over the strait to mainland Nova Scotia and Victoria General Hospital, Halifax. Nurse Heather Leblanc sat beside my stretcher in the back. We both worked at the Cheticamp hospital and I knew her not only as an R.N. in emergency but as a close friend. I felt at ease and safe with her beside me.

Michel and our son Gilles and Normand came by car later in the day. My daughter Michelle was already in Halifax, where she was studying radiology. This Victoria General was the hospital where three months earlier the woman cardiologist had refused to perform a balloon angioplasty to open my narrowed coronary artery.

By evening I was settled in bed and the nurses began to bring the meals around. A young doctor came in, someone I hadn't seen before.

"Denise Poirier?"

"That's me."

"I'm Dr. Casey."

That wasn't his real name—I can't remember his real name—but I always think back to him as Dr. Ben Casey, the handsome TV doctor of my youth who always had a special concern for his patients. He made that big, distant institution a place I wanted to be.

"Denise, your case is an interesting one."

"That's good, I guess. *I'm* very interested."

"I wanted to ask you if you'd be willing to speak to my interns in the morning."

"Me?"

"I think they'd learn something about heart disease by hearing it from you."

"You mean what a nuisance it is?"

"You're a relatively young woman. Everything they've learned inclines them to believe you shouldn't have these problems."

I didn't say anything for a minute. I expected this sort of understanding from Dr. Aucoin but not from just any doctor in a big hospital, especially *that* hospital.

"I'd be honoured," I said.

"Excellent. Thank you. Your balloon angioplasty isn't scheduled yet but they should be able to tell you when by tomorrow."

"That's good. You can count on me. I'll spill the beans."

He smiled and after a few more questions he went out. I ate a little supper and dozed off, comforted by the possibility that there were medical people who didn't think their job was to dismiss my symptoms.

I woke up and looked at my watch. It was half past midnight. I tried to sit up. Something was wrong. Incredibly, I felt the pain I'd had three mornings earlier in Cheticamp. I pushed the buzzer and after a minute a nurse came.

"It's happening," I said.

"What's happening?"

"The subendocardinal infarct."

I amazed myself I could pronounce it. She looked me, looked at the monitor, went out and came back with a new doctor. Dr. Casey had gone home.

"I'm unusual for a woman of my age," I explained.

They wheeled me to intensive care and pumped me full of morphine to wait out the long night.

We'd always been on the thin side, our family. It didn't seem to bother my brothers but it surely bothered me. When I was nineteen, I'd heard that the drug store in Inverness had a medication you could take and at the end of the treatment you'd have gained ten pounds. There was no drug store in Cheticamp and patients got their medicines directly from their doctor.

Ten pounds more. I couldn't get that out of my mind. I'd gone to see Dr. Gabriel Boudreau. I could picture his kindly old face now, even in the blinking darkness of the ICU. He'd told me to get on the scale. Ninety-eight pounds. He shook his head, sat down and looked at me.

"Denise, there's no way I'm going to give you a prescription to gain weight. I've known all you kids from birth. Maybe Wilfred and Ronald aren't typical Deveaus, but there's no doubt in my mind that you and Normand are—through and through."

I remembered looking at him round-eyed. I didn't understand.

"I wouldn't be surprised, Denise, if you and Normand had vascular problems at an early age. We have to keep an eye on you."

"What do you mean?"

"I mean that not *if* but *when* it happens, the less weight you'll be carrying the better it will be for you."

I walked out of his office, forgot about the weight medication and for years forgot anything else he told me.

Morning came at last and they did the angioplasty.

That summer was a busy one for me. Both children had jobs and expected supper on the table when their day was done. Michel had fished the lobster season in May and June and felt he'd done his duty for the year. Now, with his summer free as it had never been, he'd decided to pursue his other interests: the bar at the Royal Canadian Legion Club and the bar at the Doryman Tavern. He had friends to entertain, to be sure.

My work at the hospital was full-time work, demanding and laden with responsibility. The angioplasty was behind me and everyone assumed I was feeling great. Indeed, I *was* great, except that I was tired most of the time. After work the prospect of cleaning the house, washing the clothes and putting them away, cooking the meals—it stretched out in front of me every evening, an ordeal to be endured.

Yet I was grateful, grateful that the burden of angina had been lifted, grateful that I could go through the summer days without chest pain and shortness of breath. I certainly didn't miss going to bed and then waking up in the middle of the night in pain. And Dr. Aucoin seemed so happy that

I'd finally received treatment.

That was where my problem began. I couldn't bring myself to tell him—and I would never have told anyone else—about my arms and legs. The pain had begun to return and it was almost continuous. What would he think, after all his efforts, if I were to go back to him complaining?

I was off work one August afternoon and I knew he was away. I dropped in at the medical clinic associated with the Cheticamp Pharmacy. They had all my records. This would be a good way to test the waters without bothering Claudie.

An English-speaking doctor saw me. I'd never spoken to him before but he told me he was familiar with my file. I sat as he leafed through it sheet by sheet. There were a lot of pages. Finally he looked up.

"So?"

I explained about my arms and my legs. When I was done, he closed the file.

"Mrs. Poirier," he said. "What we find with patients like you is that you don't want to accept the fact that you're better now."

"Yeah, I do. It's good that the angina's gone. I'm very happy it's gone. But it's my legs and arms—they hurt so much."

"Mrs. Poirier, my advice to you is that you forget the whole unfortunate episode of your angina and move on with your life. How old are you now?"

"I'm thirty-nine."

"You're simply looking for twenty-year-old legs, Mrs. Poirier."

"I don't know. I just thought I should have less pain."

"Everyone has pain, madam. I think you're having trouble

with the fact you're getting older."

As I was driving home, I stopped by the side of the road. Up ahead I saw Emily Burns, who must have been sixty-five years. She was mowing her lawn. I drove past her, then home, parked the jeep, went into the garage and got out the lawn mower. I pushed it around the yard for a minute or two but my arms and legs just couldn't take it. I decided I'd just sit on the front veranda and enjoy the nice weather. The hot, late summer sun felt good on my face and the pain in my arms and legs eased a little. I looked down the hill towards the harbour. Camelle Larade, my neighbour who lived up from me was actually running up the hill towards me, pushing her little niece in a stroller. Her niece was laughing and Camelle was singing.

"Hi Denise!" she called and she laughed as she passed. I waved and held back the tears.

The seasons rolled around and then they rolled around again. Luckily for me Mama was doing well on her own at the seniors' apartment, surrounded by a group of women friends and apparently happy. I regarded this as my good luck. Michelle was in Halifax furthering her education and doing well. Gilles was in Port Hawkesbury at the Nautical Institute working towards becoming a master mariner.

Michel was still fishing lobster. During the winter he was often at the Legion, at the tavern, or at the Ski-Doo club. On those nights he wasn't home, when my day was done and the children were tucked away safely in bed. I would go to bed and fall immediately into a dreamless sleep. One night in January, Michel came home about three and I woke up briefly. I could hear him rattling beer bottles in the fridge but I pretended I was asleep. The next morning I found him sitting at the kitchen table having a beer. I made my toast and coffee. My legs were hurting badly and I said so.

"It's nothing, Denise," he said. "Stop worrying. It's nothing severe."

"Maybe not," I said.

"It's nothing real," he added.

I turned to him.

"You got in at three, Michel."

He looked at me a moment longer than necessary, then nodded.

"What's your excuse?" I asked. "You're not going to try and convince me the Ski-Doo club was open 'til three, I hope."

"No no." He took a long swallow from the bottle and set it carefully on the table. "Willie Leblanc and me were talking. Then the bartender locked up and the three of us stayed there talking 'til three."

"Until three o'clock."

"Right."

I knew he was lying. The question was: Why? For once I decided to check him out. I'd call Willie's wife, whom I knew pretty well.

I was late. I hurried out because I had a department meeting scheduled for eight. I never called Willie's wife.

In May of 1989 I drove up with Gloria Leblanc to the Victoria General Hospital in Halifax for a follow-up angiogram. By then that huge place had become as familiar as my own Sacred Heart in Cheticamp. I waited uneasily in a cubicle in the cardiac department for about fifteen minutes. Here at least was a chance to talk about my legs with someone truly knowledgeable, someone caring. The door opened. It was Dr O'Hara.

"You," she said. Her blue eyes seemed to pierce me. She had her black hair pulled straight back. "Hello," she added.

"Look—" I wasn't going to let her get started. "Look, I'm not concerned about my heart and I'm not interested in this angiogram. It's your department that called me for a follow-up. I'm here and I'll go through with it."

She looked at me. "Right," she said.

"But since I *am* here, do you think it might be possible that somebody could have a look at my legs?"

"Your legs?" Like they weren't part of me.

"My legs. They hurt awful bad when I walk and even at night when I'm in bed. And my arms. Maybe somebody could have a look before I'm discharged?"

"Mrs Poirier," she said. "I've seen you a number of times and, believe me, I know your case."

"Well, that's what I mean."

"I understand you very well—and people like you."

Oh oh. 'People like you' didn't sound good.

"You've got two factors active here. First of all, you like being sick."

"Me? How can I like being sick? I got a busy job. I work for a hospital too, you know. I got a husband and two kids to look after."

"One—" Her hand was at her side but I could see she was actually wagging her finger. "One, you like being sick and, two, you hate your job."

"Who told you that?"

"I don't know what you do at a hospital but I'm sure it isn't pleasant. Maybe we shouldn't blame you, but none of this has anything to do with a thirty-nine-year-old woman who thinks she's dying from heart disease."

For once, I couldn't think of a thing to say.

They performed the angiogram later the same day. As I lay in the recovery room an intense coldness passed over me. I began to shiver and the blankets didn't help. It was May but I felt as though my life was Cheticamp on a winter day, when the storm fronts roll in from the ocean to smother the houses in darkness. That's also the time when the smallest patch of sunlight seems most brilliant.

They had found an occlusion—a blockage—in the artery of my right leg. The surgeons—not Dr. O'Hara—repaired it on the third day and I remained in the Victoria General for another week. After the operation, Dr. Kinley, the head cardiovascular surgeon, came to see me. He was a man in his late fifties, short sandy hair mixed with a little tinge of gray. His face was gentle. He spoke softly and seriously and listened carefully to my answers.

"Well," he said finally. "My intention had been to create a bypass around the occlusion but when I saw the condition of your arteries, I decided to remove what plaque I could and leave you be."

"That's not good, right?"

"We're going to be doing a series of tests—you probably expected that—but from what I can see already, the condition of your arteries is extremely rare for a person of your age."

"All in my mind, right?"

He smiled a bit at my irony.

"Not. I'm sure everything you report is quite real and my job is to extend your life as far as possible by looking after you now *and* later."

It might seem bad news coming from a senior physician. I held the bed covers tightly and said nothing. He couldn't know it, but my response was a wave of relief. He believed me. He was the shaft of sunlight that found its way through an otherwise overcast sky.

"The blood pressure in your arms and legs is far too low."

"I ate too many frites, no?"

Now he laughed.

"Mrs. Poirier, don't let anyone make you feel guilty. Even if you'd lived a really unhealthy lifestyle—and I don't see that you have—you're just too young for this."

"It's not my fault? Is that what you're saying?"

"It's not your fault."

"It's not in my mind?" I experienced an almost fierce sense of justice being done, even if there were no real culprits.

"No. It's probably in your genes."

"Ah. Those genes."

"I'm afraid so. When we're done with you here I'll be sending a report to Dr. Aucoin. I believe you see him."

"Dr. Aucoin? I work in the same hospital as him."

"Well then, when you see him next, tell him Dr. Kinley

says you have advanced chronic peripheral vascular disease and I'll be telling him all about it."

"You tell him about it." It was beginning to sink in. This was all real, not a temporary problem or some sort of mental thing.

"I'd like you to come back here in August and we'll have another look at these legs."

"Sure." I felt in good hands.

"Remember—" These were the man's last words that day. "Whatever we find, I'm here to look after you."

When he was gone, I actually felt warm. The nightmare was over. I could face the disease because at last my experience made sense and my mind could get some rest.

I n August, Dr. Kinley was disappointed to find the blood pressure in my legs was still low. He began a series of trials with various medications but by December, when I had failed to respond to the best drugs available, he would make the decision that would save my life—and change it out of all recognition. He advised me to quit my job and told me that he would recommend that I be placed on permanent disability. Michel sat with me as the good doctor wished me luck and told me to enjoy the rest of my life as best I could. I prided myself that I held my tears in the face of such news but I cried all the way home to Cheticamp.

I was forty-two and suddenly retired. My job—my wellspring of pride, self-confidence, self-esteem, usefulness and accomplishment—was gone. Now I would cook, shop, clean. I would be a housewife again.

I met my friend Anasthasie Crowdis one June afternoon

at the co-op store. Anasthasie was in the insurance business. She'd just left her office and was still in her suit and it was great to see her. We stopped and talked and I was glad she never mentioned my jeans and T-shirt, and glad she couldn't see the small flame of envy that was burning inside me.

130

An Unexpected Visitor

That winter of 1991. There are winters that just don't go well, winters when no fine blue skies cheer your heart. The cold stings your face and the weeks go by and the sun doesn't offer you any hint of spring-time. By January, the Christmas trees are all tossed out in the snow and the parties all forgotten and, winters like that, the wind blows straight in from the sea and even the island doesn't quite protect us. Cheticantins huddle in their houses and wait.

Our daughter Michelle was working now at the regional hospital in Kentville, Nova Scotia. Our son Gilles was still enrolled at the Nautical Institute in Port Hawkesbury, pursuing his master mariner's degree. Michel and I were alone together. He spent his days building and repairing his traps. I cooked and kept our house and visited Mama.

A January morning—a rare clear, sunny day—there was a knock on the kitchen door and Normand poked his head in.

"Come in quick and shut that door."

He had taken his boots off in the porch and was bent over brushing snow from the cuffs of his pants.

"I haven't finished the coffee so you're just in time." I put the pot on the stove and turned around.

"Normand. What's the matter?"

"What?"

"What's wrong?"

"Nothing. I'm just on my way over to see Claudie."

"Normand, you don't look right."

"Yeah, yeah. Well, I've lost fifteen pounds since last Friday. That's what it is."

I sat down in my chair at the kitchen table. "Fifteen pounds?"

"It's this pain in the back of my neck that's bothering me, really. And here in my side at the hip. It hurts."

I looked at him but he didn't meet my eyes. I thought he looked pale.

"You're going to see Claudie?"

"In about twenty minutes."

I could hear the coffee starting to bubble.

I generally went to visit Mama every day and that day was no exception. She and I went up together to the hospital about three, when we knew the workers were on break, just to see the people we'd worked with—many of the same people. I'd started to get past feeling so sorry for myself, no longer the working professional. I thought more and more often about the fact that I was alive. When everyone else had gone back on shift, Mama and I stayed for a while at the cafeteria table. I kept thinking about Normand, but I wasn't going to mention his visit.

"I often wonder," I started. "I often wonder how you cope with the fact that three of your children are in, you know, sort of bad shape. Does it bother you?"

She didn't show any surprise. She knew I asked this sort of question.

"It didn't all happen in one day, Denise. Everything crept up slowly on me, starting with your father. Me, I made up my mind a long time ago I'd accept whatever was thrown my way. I'll tell you the truth, Denise, I feel fortunate and grateful that Ronald has been spared. Up to now, anyway."

Normand called about suppertime to say they were admitting him to the hospital for some tests. He went in the next day and I stopped by to see him.

"I think it's just a damn bug," he said.

He called me to pick him up two days later. When he got in the car, he lit a cigarette.

"Nothing much showed up," he said. "There might be a little problem with the pancreas. They'll look into it."

"Is that all?"

"It's nothing much, really. But Denise, look, until I get better, I wonder if I could stay with you and Michel? This thing's sort of set me back a bit."

"Of course."

"It wouldn't bother you?"

"Of course not, Normand. It would be great to have you."

We drove home in silence, me with a cold pit in my stomach.

Michel liked Normand and was always kind to him. When he got home that night and saw my brother settled in with us, he just said, "Fine." He went to the fridge and got two beers, one for Normand. He plunked himself down on the sofa and took a few swallows.

"How long you going to say?" he asked.

"Not long," Normand said.

"Long as you like." Michel said. He lit a cigarette and after a while he got up, turned on the TV, came back and stretched himself out.

"It's your place as far as I'm concerned," he said.

Over the next few weeks it seemed to me Normand was getting worse every day. He started spitting up blood and eating less and less. He told me he was passing blood in his stool and I could see he was losing more weight. He was taking Tylenol all day long.

He had a lot of friends and they often came to visit. They'd sit around and talk about Normand's crazy escapades with Claudie Aucoin and the time he was driving his Ski-Doo at full speed and couldn't stop in time and crashed it into the frozen pier. Sometimes I'd hear them laughing but I never heard anyone say anything about his condition. It was like something agreed. Finally Claudie showed up one afternoon and I was glad. He'll get Normand back into the hospital, I thought, but Normand told him nothing and Claudie didn't ask. I was starting to feel a terrible tension in me. I couldn't talk about it to anyone on the phone because Normand would have heard me.

Michel's routine didn't change. He still came and went as he pleased. He drank beer every day but he was rarely actually drunk. He'd settled into a pattern: he'd drink beer every day for about three weeks, then go overboard for days, make himself sick, then go back to his regular drinking. For me it was normal.

When Normand wasn't in his room sleeping, he lay on the couch where Michel was used to sit, watching TV. Michel now occupied the chair where I usually sat. If he missed his couch, he never grumbled.

We had a black cast iron wood stove and Normand took over feeding it. Then one Sunday afternoon he backed up from the stove and sat down on the sofa hard.

"Denise, I just put my last piece of wood in that stove."

"You too warm, Normand?"

"No. My neck, it hurts too much. That was the last piece."

From the doorway, I looked at him from behind, so still on the sofa. He didn't say anything else.

On January 14, Tante Antoinette died. She was Papape's sister but I didn't go to her funeral because I didn't want to leave Normand alone. Tante Martine came from Montreal to her sister's wake. She telephoned and talked to Normand. He just talked about Tante Antoinette. When he hung up, he sat there a minute.

"Maybe I should have told her that was the last time I'd be talking to her," he said. His tone was matter-of-fact.

Here was the opening I'd been longing for.

"Normand." I went over and sat on the couch. "I'm glad you said that. I can't be with you day after day and pretend you're going to get well. I can't keep it up. I know as well as you that you're not going to get out of this alive."

He looked at me, made a very small smile.

"But how does it feel to know you're going to die?" I asked.

He must have expected sooner or later he'd get that question from me.

"Denise, I'm so uncomfortable and I'm in so much pain, to tell you the truth, I wish I could die right now while we're talking. I know you found it odd that I didn't tell Claudie but I knew it was too late. There's nothing he can do to help me."

"You sure, Normand?"

"Denise, Claudie knows it too."

Of course. "Are you scared?"

He thought about that a moment.

"It can't be that bad. Everyone goes through it one day or another. Don't worry about me, Denise, I'll be fine. I'm just hoping there's going to be someone on the other side to make it interesting. I'm hoping Winston will be there, at least."

His friend Winston Merry had died a few months earlier from a fall downstairs in his own house.

Every morning after his bath, Normand got himself into clean panamas and I'd wash his hair in the sink. I thought if he was fresh every morning it would make him feel better during the day. He seemed to be uncomfortable with it, though, and one morning he started crying out in pain while I was working in the shampoo. I stood back, feeling helpless.

"I won't do this anymore, Normand," I said. "It's hurting me as much as it's hurting you."

So there was no more hair washing. Still, each day I'd ask him what he'd like to eat and one night I cooked him his favourite chowder made with all kinds of seafood—cod, scallops, shrimps, lobster, crab and clams. He ate a bit, nodded, set down his spoon slowly. A few days later he was readmitted at the Cheticamp hospital and they sent him to Sydney. I went to see him at the hospital there and was surprised to learn that he was allowed to smoke in his room. Not me—I wasn't a patient—so Normand would slip me his cigarette. I didn't like the idea of puffing on his cigarette—passing cigarettes from my lips to the lips of someone who looked like a dead man—but I couldn't bear to hurt his feelings.

The last day I spent with him at the Sydney hospital, we used our time to discuss what I was to do after he was gone. Then we said our goodbyes and I gathered my things quickly.

"Denise." I stopped. "Listen, do me a favour, will you? Even with the morphine I can't stand the pain anymore. On your way out, stop at the nursing station and tell the nurse to have a doctor take me in the O.R. and cut my head off. Will you do that?"

I gave him my best smile. "Consider it done," I said. "You know you could always depend on me to get things done."

From Sydney they transferred him to the Victoria General Hospital in Halifax. I called Claudie and told him how a doctor in Sydney had explained to me that the cancer was eating at the bone in the back of Normand's neck. Claudie had a hard time with this and the following day he called me back to say he'd been up to visit Normand and helped him with his breakfast. The cancer had spread all over.

I called Wilfred and Ronald. Ronald came home and Mama came to stay with us. Wilfred and his daughter Lies went to Halifax to be with Normand. I was too exhausted but I called him that morning and asked him how things were going.

"I spit up an awful lot of blood this morning," he said. "The end is near. You know that."

I'd been debating with myself whether I should ask a question or not. It was the sort of question I was prone to ask. This was my last chance.

"Normand, you remember all the talks we had about death through the years and how we were okay with it? Remember those?"

"Yes."

"Now that it's here, if you were given the choice of two more months to live, but you had to live them in the exact condition you're in now, would you take them?" I knew before I asked. What could be worse than this awful suffering? Let death come, the sooner the better.

There was a silence.

"Normand?"

"Yeah, Denise. I hear you. Listen, I'm still telling you I'm not scared to die. I'm completely okay with it."

"Right."

"But...but yes, I'd take those two months."

I was sorry I'd asked but it was too late for that.

"Normand, I love you so much and I'll miss you so much. Goodbye, Normand."

"Goodbye, Denise."

When Papape died, Mama had bought a double burial plot in the Cheticamp Parish Cemetery so she would be with him when her turn came. The big headstone with Papape's inscription on one side had hers on the other. But Mama didn't want Normand to be buried alone. She told the funeral director to put Normand's coffin beside Papape. The funeral director suggested they put Normand further down but she didn't want that. She wanted Normand beside Papape. She said she'd be cremated and her urn of ashes would be buried on top of Papape. So Normand's date of birth and death were inscribed beside his father's and they were laid side by side.

Families Crossing

The Deveaus

Joseph and Olive

Joseph and Olive

Papape's father, my pépère Joseph Deveau, married my mémère Olive Aucoin in 1912. Between the years 1913 and 1932 the couple had fourteen children and they brought them up in Belle Marche, near Cheticamp. Pépère Joseph died of a heart attack at age sixty-five. Mémère Olive died in her seventies of congestive heart failure. Of their fourteen children, ten have so far died of heart disease. Let me tell you quickly about nine of them.

Pierre Paul Deveau

Oncle Pierre Paul was married to Bernadette, who was a favourite tante of mine. He was a kind and gentle person who enjoyed spending his time off with his family. When he was a young lad still living with his parents in Belle Marche, he had an old bicycle. As often as he could, he would visit his older sister, Helene, who was married with children and lived eight miles away. That meant pedaling sixteen miles on gravel roads. In those days of no car or telephone, this was the only way their mother could get news of Helene and her children. Pierre Paul was working at Dean Evans' coal mine in St. Rose, a village near neighbouring Margaree. He and Tante Bernadette lived in Cheticamp and had three daughters: Honora, Karen, and Yolande.

Oncle Pierre Paul had a heart attack when he was thirty-nine, but he survived. One night when he was about forty-five he called out to Karen, who was in her room doing her homework. She assumed he just wanted her to refill the coal scuttle. He called again. Karen went in and found him out of breath, sweating, and blue in the face. He was hospitalized but to no avail.

Lionel Deveau

Oncle Lionel worked in an office in Montreal and never married. When he was in his thirties his doctors told him that he had a heart problem but there was nothing they could do.

Oncle Lionel always spent his summer vacation in Cheticamp and I remember how he loved our family gatherings and especially Acadian fiddle music. For my wedding, he gave me a big Pyrex dish and cover sitting in a fancy heavy silver platter. Every time I cleaned the cupboards, I had to spend time polishing the tarnished silver. One day—I remember it was a Thursday in the spring of 1969—I was cleaning up and decided I'd just had enough of polishing that platter so I threw it out and kept the Pyrex dish and cover.

That weekend, Oncle Lionel decided to go to his Montreal office to finish off a project but when he got there, he found the light bulb above his desk was burned out. Nobody was around so he stood on a chair and stretched his arms up to reach the bulb and fell down dead. He was forty three. I felt so guilty about the silver platter but the garbage man had come and gone Friday.

Damien Deveau

Oncle Damien lived in Halifax and worked in a men's clothing store. He married Delores and they had two children, Judy and Michael. I remember the family having Sunday dinner at our house in Cheticamp only once and unfortunately I never got to know them well.

In 1968 Oncle Damien had a heart attack at home. He stumbled to his bed and an ambulance was called. Uncle Damien's pain was so intense, his grip on the metal headboard railings twisted them out of shape before he died. He was forty-eight.

His daughter Judy died at age fifty-three.

Fabien Deveau

Oncle Fabien worked as a chef in a motel restaurant in Halifax. He and Tante Agnes had no children. In 1974 he got to worrying on account of the recent fates of his brothers. He went to see his doctor for a check-up and the doctor assured him he was in A-1 condition. After supper a few weeks later, he told Tante Agnes that he felt a bit nauseated. He  said he was pretty sure that if he could get rid of his supper he'd be okay. Tante Agnes called an ambulance anyway but he died on the way to the hospital.

Oncle Fabien was the only Deveau to have an autopsy. The report said that his heart and arteries were like those of a man well over eighty. He was fifty-three.

Pauline Deveau

Tante Pauline was in charge of a motel cigar and gift shop in Halifax. She never married but took an early retirement and moved back to Cheticamp to live with her widowed sister, Tante Marie. Of course she was worried because of her brothers but she'd quit smoking when she was younger and she took her daily walks and watched her diet. She was a really healthy person.

At suppertime on the 29th of April, 1986, she dropped dead on the front steps of the Cheticamp post office when she was going in to mail a letter. She was fifty-seven.

Marie Chiasson (née Deveau)

Tante Marie married Oncle Joseph Chiasson and lived in Belle Marche, the part of Cheticamp where she was born. They had no children but always had a dog who would do tricks for a homemade cookie. Tante Marie loved to pick berries and every year she make sure my deep freezer was full of wild strawberries, blueberries and cranberries. In the summer she gave me loads of fresh vegetables from her garden.

Tante Marie told me that when she walked, she often experienced chest pain that radiated to her jaw. Her doctor gave her nitro pills to put under the tongue and wanted her to see a specialist in Halifax but she refused. She died from a heart attack while picking wild fruit. Blueberries. She was sixty-seven.

Henri Deveau

Oncle Henri was married to Tante Catherine Roach. They lived in Halifax. Oncle Henri was head cook on a CNR train. He retired back to Belle Marche and moved in with his widowed sister, Tante Marie.

When they were all much younger, Oncle Henri and Tante Catherine and their three children—Linda, Donald and Terry—would come to Cheticamp to visit at my Oncle Dominique's. I remember Linda best. We were both four years old the first time we met and she looked to me like a fairy princess. All of us Cheticamp cousins were dressed in country cotton dresses and plain brown shoes but Linda was wearing a silky pink flared dress with dainty pink socks and shiny patent leather shoes. She spoke to us in French with an English accent and she was just naturally a kind hearted and humble child. When she grew older and could spend a couple of weeks at Uncle Dominique's, she brought a small two-wheel bicycle. We'd never seen anything like it and she let all us country cousins take turns whenever we liked, which was all the time.

When Oncle Henri moved back to live at Tante Marie's, he'd come over to visit me often and bring me cucumbers and other vegetables from his garden. I remember one afternoon when he was seventy-five we got to talking about his poor brothers and sisters and he said how lucky he'd been to be so healthy. A week or so later he was out for a walk on a bright January morning and started feeling weird. He stopped into a house close by to sit down and the man living there called an ambulance.

At least it was a quick death. His daughter, dear Linda, had to have coronary angioplasty when she was fifty-two.

Dominique Deveau

Oncle Dominique was married to Tante Jeanne Roach and lived in the Belle Marche house where he'd been brought up. By the time he took over the farm, Pépère and Mémère had moved to Halifax. Oncle Dominique was a hard-working farmer and Tante Jeanne worked just as hard as he did. They had five children: Clarence, Yvette, Claudia, Bruno, and Pamela.

Oncle Dominique lived for years with his heart condition, with shortness of breath and ankles always swollen. His suffering troubled me. I began to think that those who died quickly fared better than those who lingered, but for better or worse Oncle Dominique died at seventy-three. In many ways he reminded me of my own father: even the simplest chore had become a big struggle for him.

Dominique's son Clarence was in his fifties when he developed a heart condition. Last I heard he was doing okay.

Antoinette Roach (née Deveau)

Tante Antoinette married Oncle Joseph Roach and they had four children: Marie-Agnes, Lubie, Claude, and Malthide. They had a farm and a garden and Oncle Joseph worked for the

Department of Highways in Cheticamp. They had taken over Oncle Joseph's old homestead in Belle Marche, just a few houses down the road from Oncle Dominique. Tante Antoinette was lucky with her health. In her mid-seventies, the doctors fitted her with a pacemaker. She did well with it and was feeling particularly good one January morning when she was seventy-seven. She called her daughter Malthide, who lived across the street from her, and asked her to come down to pick up some fresh bread for supper. Later in the afternoon Malthide did go down and found the bread still in the oven and Aunt Antoinette passed away in the rocking chair.

My cousin, Malthide, is married to Daniel Bourgeois, who is also my cousin on my mother's side. My cousin Lubie had coronary angioplasty in his fifties. He's still okay.

The Bourgeois
Cyril and Louise

Mama's father, Cyril Bourgeois, married Louise Boudreau in 1918 and between 1919 and 1933 they brought up eight children in Cheticamp. Of these eight, four died directly or indirectly because of circulatory problem. Let me mention three.

Willie Arthur Bourgeois

Oncle Willie Arthur was born August 25 in 1923. He died April 15, 1994 at the age of 70. He married Tante Marie Josephine Aucoin and together they raised two children, Yvon and Ginette. They lived in Cheticamp and Oncle Willie Arthur worked on the freighter *Rio* with his father, Captain Cyril Bourgeois. Later he worked as a mechanic at his brother-in-law's garage. From his late fifties on, Oncle Willie underwent numerous operations due to peripheral vascular disease. He had grafts of the aorta and leg arteries done a number of times. Then his right leg was cut off below the knee. His left leg was amputated on three different occasions. It was first cut above the knee, then it was cut halfway to the top, and lastly it was cut to the very top. His circulation was so poor that they had to graft skin from his other leg to patch up the wound.

Louis Leo Bourgeois

Oncle Louis Leo was born February 12, 1933 and died in August of 2001 at the age of 66. He married Tante Marie Stella Lefort and had three children: Francine, Pauline, and Cyril. I was very close to Oncle Louis Leo and

Tante Marie Stella and they were the couple who stood with Michel and me at our wedding. Louis Leo was manager of the co-op store in Cheticamp and later moved his family to Montreal and worked in an office. In his early fifties he developed occlusions in his legs and aorta and a couple of years later his carotid arteries were repaired. The last  years of his life were spent in physical misery. I still recall him walking painfully with the help of a cane.

Wilfred Bourgeois

Oncle Wilfred was born August 22, 1926. He married Tante Therese and together they raised three girls: Stella, Annette, and Michelle. They first lived in Cheticamp and later moved to Montreal. Wilfred was the first mate on oil tankers for Canada Steamship Lines but he eventually left the sea and took  a job as traffic officer at the Port of Montreal. He loved his three girls so much. I remember him lovingly teasing them every chance he got. In 1974 he had a triple bypass, took his retirement in 1987, and died in March of 1992.

Of the fourteen afflicted children of my four grandparents, I've described twelve. Many of them married into nearby families and four of my father's siblings married into a single neighbouring family, the Roach family of Belle Marche. That was often how it was in our little island of

Acadian life. But when Papape married Mama in 1944, nei-ther of them had any reason to think about what lay hidden in their genes. They were thinking about starting a family and making a better life in the new post-war world that was just dawning. The insights that come with looking back are the privilege of the survivors.

Of Moving and Jigging

ormand left me his house in his will. He'd been so proud of it, the tidy bungalow on the hill with a living room that looked out over the sea. I was the only member of our immediate family who had remained in Cheticamp and I was honoured at the bequest, though I didn't want to live in Normand's house. People started calling me about it right away, offering to buy it, and I was ready to sell. Michel could hardly believe his ears.

"Denise," he pleaded. "Look at it. Look where Normand built it. We could really see the ocean from there. We could see boats coming in when they're still miles out."

"I don't care," I said. "I don't have the energy to face a move."

"Come on, Denise. You know I'll do the work. Think about sitting up there on our couch and watching storms raging out there on the ocean."

"I've thought about it but I like our house. I like our neighbours."

He followed me into the kitchen. "But Normand's place is on a way, way bigger piece of land," he said. "And look at the garage—it's way bigger."

"We're not farmers, Michel."

Michel wasn't a loud man or an angry one and he let the matter drop. Probably better he did, because I'd been frustrated with him since Normand's death. For all my ignoring it, his drinking got to me. I wasn't going to budge about the house.

My son Gilles came home to visit and surprised me by intervening.

"Mama," he said when we were alone one morning in February. "Can I tell you what I think about Normand's house?"

"Of course you can."

"I think you're being a bit mean and selfish."

"Gilles. Are you kidding?"

"No. I'm serious. I think Papape has a point."

"Really?" I was surprised because I knew Gilles harboured some resentment towards Michel. "You think I'm supposed to leave my home so your father can have a bigger garage?"

"It's a nice house, Mom, but it's not about Dad. It's about Normand. Oncle Normand would be so disappointed if he knew you were selling his house."

"Normand? Disappointed?" I was standing there, holding onto the back of a chair, looking at him.

"He thought you'd want to have his house," Gilles said.

"Normand? Why would he?" I was trying to sound rational but I wasn't doing a very good job, judging by the sad way Gilles was looking at me. I was struggling to discover my real feelings "I…I just keep thinking that he'd…that I'd be thinking about him in every room."

"Mom. It would be like Normand was still with you. He was thinking about you and now you'd be thinking about him. That's not so bad."

The next afternoon, my niece and godchild Angela called me to say if I ever wanted to move, she and her husband Alexi would love to buy our place. A lot of our friends pitched in, Michel made sure I didn't exert myself, and our furnishings began their journey some five houses distance to our new home. Me, I just sat in the living room of our house and then the living room of Normand's house and decided what to keep and what to get rid of. Out the living room window, down the slope, across the road and beyond the harbour, the sea was a mass of ice as far as the eye could see. No storms were raging.

We settled in. Michel rented a government fisherman's shed on the island. He stored his lobster and crab traps there and did the repairs on the traps during the winter months. His buoys he kept in the garage by the house. In the fall of each year he'd give them a new coat of paint and we'd sit and talk while he was painting. The big door was open and we could watch the traffic and the people and the boats going by. Bit by bit, I remembered that I was happy again.

Now Michel and I joined the passing parade of generations. Michelle married Jerry Lutz, an ambulance worker in Kentville, Nova Scotia and in May of 1992, the phone rang with the news that she had given birth to our first grandchild, Matthew. Life can't deliver more exciting news than that to a person like me. We visited back and forth for a couple of years and then Michelle divorced Jerry and moved back in with us. My attachment to Matthew grew deeper over the months that followed. Then Michelle got a job as an MRI technologist at the Cape Breton Regional Hospital in

Sydney and Michel and I were alone again except for a golden retriever we named Prince. He was our new baby. We'd go in the National Park with him or Michel would take him for long walks. One summer morning in 1996 Michel took Prince to check the boat and Prince decided to come back home on his own and was struck by a car. He died at the bottom of our driveway.

During those years I'd often fly to Montreal to visit my brother Ronald and my Tante Martine and cousin Marie Rose. Michel would stay home, in part because he was afraid of flying, but he'd call me every night and ask me if I'd be returning home. He'd be worried I'd left him. Crazy, I thought. He kept telling me how much he loved and missed me. I never had to say that. Everyone—even Michel—knew how much I loved him.

In August of 1994 Mama entered the Foyer Père Fiset home for seniors in Cheticamp. Lots of her friends were already there and she knew all the workers. They looked after her baths, her meals, her medication and her clothes. Still, I was concerned about how she would be treated. I couldn't be there to watch every minute but as it happened, she left the phone off the hook by accident one night and I listened while a worker helped her get ready for bed. I couldn't believe what I was hearing: not callousness or briskness or crisp professionalism, but gentleness and kindness. When I was small and putting my dolls to bed, I'd spoken to them like that.

It was a new phase in our lives, yet in many respects, everything remained the same for Mama and me. During the day, we'd often go together to the Gabriel restaurant for lunch or to visit her sister Marguerite-Marie who lived across from the Co-op grocery store. She even visited Wilfred once in

Shediac, N.B. for a week.

We passed our time in simple ways, Michel and I. In the fall he'd buy wood for the fireplace and I'd go with him for the drive up to Middle River and watch him load the truck, drive back home, unload it and cord it. In the evenings, we'd sit and watch the fire together. I enjoyed the process even though I was of no help. Since he wouldn't fly, we'd some- times take short trips to Sydney or Halifax or P.E.I. or by sea through the ice to Newfoundland. The whole period had a strange autumnal feel about it. Michel and I were alone but together. This after all was what I'd always wanted.

There was the dark side, of course: the drinking. The man was a good provider and neither violent nor strict, but the children resented him from an early age. They knew they couldn't depend on him for anything and they were always worried that when they had friends over he'd show up drunk. And crazily in love as I still was, there was a dark side to my own feelings, as surfaced one very cold night in the dead of winter—it might have been around midnight—when I woke up to find Michel wasn't there, as usual. I didn't turn on any lights because I knew my way to the bathroom but I hap- pened to look out the window as I went through the kitchen. Far across the field, lit by the moon and silhouetted against the snow, I could see him staggering his way home from the Legion. He fell. I could see he couldn't get up. I watched for a moment, then went to the bathroom and returned to bed. I learned the following day that our next door neighbour, who was also at the Legion, had found him and brought him safely home. I loved Michel but if he had died there in the snow, I'd have pretended I knew nothing. I never felt respon- sible for his actions.

But that was the depths of a winter night. The countless times we went cod fishing together were more typical of Michel and me. When he had done with the lobster and crab about the middle of August, he'd leave the *Mighty Matthew* at the wharf until he stored it for the winter season in a vast building where fishermen could work on their boats without worries about the wild winter storms of Cheticamp. On warm calm days we'd drive down from our house to the wharf about four in the afternoon. We always dressed in comfortable old clothes. Getting out of my business outfits would be a special treat for me while I was still working at the hospital and later after my forced retirement. It was great to be doing something outside. Michel might have had a few beers during the day but he was generally sober on these expeditions and we always brought four more beers with us—two each. Sometimes we'd pick up fish and chips to eat on our way to the fishing grounds. (It seemed like Cheticantins could never have too much fish.) Other times I'd bring sandwiches and treats that we'd eat when we took a break from jigging.

The *Mighty Matthew* had a thirty-foot fiberglass hull and could make about twelve miles an hour. Some fishing boats were dirty but Michel was naturally a neat person who would keep the boat as clean as I kept our house. Once I was safely aboard, he'd untie the lines and start the diesel engine. We'd push off from the wharf, steer towards the mouth of Cheticamp's harbour and from there cross into a different world: the vastness of the Gulf of St. Lawrence, an arm of the North Atlantic. I'd breathe the sea air and look back at our house and the houses of our neighbours. Everything appeared orderly from the distance: the freshly cut green lawns, the houses, the shops, the sweeping mountains behind them.

There was no trace of the messy lives of some of my friends and neighbours. Then I'd turn and look ahead as we passed Cheticamp Island and all you could see was ocean stretching away to the horizon.

The jigging grounds were three-quarters of a mile off shore from the National Park and I could make out some of the curving roads on the big slope of the mountain. We were perhaps three miles from the wharf. Michel would take bearings from this point or that point and mix the bearings with his experience and arrive at the best fishing spots. Other boats would often cluster nearby. Our neighbours, Paul and Marie Rose, enjoyed jigging cod as much as Michel and I did, and sometimes the men would bring the boats side by side and we'd joke back and forth and compare our catches. We'd see boats filled with tourists and sometimes we'd spot schools of pilot whales. The first time I'd seen them, years earlier, seven or eight were still far off but rushing towards us in a straight line. I gasped in fear. At the last moment they veered to the right and passed close to the boat—powerful, dark, frightening.

"Nothing to be afraid of," Michel had said. "Just whales minding their own business."

Before going out, Michel would have made up a square frame of one-inch-wide wood a foot on each side. He used maybe seventy-five feet of strong clear thin nylon line and knotted one end of the line to the frame. He wound the line around the frame until he got to the end and he'd attach that end to a jigger—an eight-inch long piece of steel with three prongs at the end of it. We'd unroll our line and let the jigger go to the bottom, then bring it up about a foot. Then we jigged. The cod we were after were about eighteen to twenty-four inches and whoever caught the first one, Michel would then cut off little pieces to bait the prongs. Towards the end of the day, he'd skin, gut, and fillet the catch to remove all the bones. The taste of fresh fish can't be compared to the fish sold in stores and what we didn't eat I'd freeze right away so we'd have some all winter long. I'd give a lot away because we'd always have more than we needed.

When we were done, perhaps eight in the evening, I'd sometimes just sit and look. To the west, the sun would be touching the horizon and the sea, so endless seeming, would be smeared with light. But beyond that horizon, Prince Edward Island was just out of sight, and the Îles de la Madeleine were to the north and Newfoundland to the east. These were the places I knew. Taken all together, they made my world, a world with Cheticamp at its still centre.

The boat would shift softly with the movement of the water. A few gulls would cry out overhead. Michel would busy himself with the fish. Perhaps we'd exchange a word or two as a deep indigo spread across the sky and a few stars appeared.

The Last Secret

ate August, 1996. Michel came home one day at noontime. I could see he'd been drinking. In fact he'd been drinking more heavily than ever for the past year. I was feeling the strain.

He sat heavily at the kitchen table.

"Let's take the ferry to Newfoundland," he said. "What do you think? Take a vacation there for a few days."

We'd been to Newfoundland many times, partly because we couldn't go anywhere that involved flying.

"You go," I said. "I'm happy to stay home and relax."

"Come on, Denise. Come on. Let's go have some fun."

"It would be plenty fun for me to get a break from your drinking."

"Come on."

"I'm serious."

He dropped his head down a bit, the way he did when he'd been drinking and wasn't happy about something.

"I'll go anyway," he said.

"Have a good time," I said. "Take the truck and leave me the jeep."

He packed up and left. When he was gone, I found myself in a turmoil of anger. I could hardly tell why. It just shouldn't be like this, I felt. I didn't know what, exactly. After all, I'd told him to go by himself, but it didn't matter. I was mad. I thought about how he'd never met a drinker he didn't like but was always talking about how bad dope was and how bad dope smokers were. I looked through the phone book for a name in Belle Marche. I knew the man's wife.

An hour later, a car pulled into the driveway and this man came to the door and gave me an envelope with three joints in it. Somehow, the sight of those joints on our kitchen table gave me a sort of thrill. After supper, I drew a hot bubble bath and settled into its depth.

When the water started to cool, I got out, dressed in my warm nightgown and got into bed with the marijuana and my book. This would be a new experience and one I would have all by myself. I lay on my side to read and smoked the first joint the way you'd smoke a regular cigarette, inhaling deeply. When it was done I lay there waiting for the high, that great high I'd heard so much about but had never experienced. Then I noticed my heart was beating faster. Was that right? I began to feel nauseated. I didn't remember anyone mentioning that. My heart began to race now and I became alarmed. I decided to get up but discovered I could not: I was paralyzed. My book dropped to the floor. I knew I was in trouble and would have to call for an ambulance. I looked at the telephone on my bedside table but couldn't reach for it. For maybe the first time in my life, I was sure I was going to die. The physical discomfort was overwhelming. My head was facing to the side and I formed the desperate idea that if I threw up, I'd get some relief. For a long time—I have no idea how long—I thought longingly of vomiting. Finally I did. The paralysis lifted slowly and I moved to the other side of the bed. I remember noticing that my heartbeat was back to normal. I fell to sleep.

The next afternoon, when I'd cleaned up and pulled myself together, I called my cousin and dear friend, Paulette Leblanc, to come over. She lived at the Oceanview Motel and was at the door in five minutes. I put on the coffee and we sat down. I told her Michel was in Newfoundland but I switched topics right away to talk to her about how their business was doing. As we were talking, the phone rang. It was Wilfred's wife, Marie-France. She asked me if things were going well and I told her Michel was drinking and gone away on his own. It's odd that I worded it like that, since I'd chosen to stay home, but a strange sense of grievance was bubbling up inside me. There was no doubt Marie France could hear the resentment in my voice.

"I…I hope everything's okay," she said. "I mean, every-thing's always great between you and Michel."

"No," I said. I looked at Paulette, who was watching me from the kitchen table. "No. I wouldn't say it was great."

There was a pause on the other end of the line.

"Because…?"

"Because I'm tired of the drinking."

"Of course. Of course. Is there anything else, Denise? Anything besides the drinking?"

"No. Just the drinking."

"Okay."

"Just the drinking."

"Okay, Denise."

"What do you mean, Marie France?"

"Nothing."

I looked over again at Paulette.

"Is there something I'm supposed to know?"

"No."

"Why did you ask me that question?"

"I just asked out of the blue, Denise."

"There's nothing else?"

"No, Denise."

"Denise?"

That was Paulette. She was looking straight at me now.

"Hang up the phone, Denise"

"What?"

"Hang up the phone and I'll tell you what Marie France means."

I must have stood there for some long seconds. Finally I said, "Marie France, I better go now."

"I'm sorry, Denise," I heard Marie France say.

"I have to go now, " I said.

I went back to the table and sat down.

"What is it?" I said.

Paulette lifted her head up a little, as though she was preparing to take a dive at the deep end of the pool. She made a slow exhalation. "It's Michel," she said. "And it's not the drinking."

"It's a woman," I said.

"Women."

So there it was.

"How long has it been going on?"

Paulette didn't answer right away. She took another breath instead.

"Always," she finally said.

I didn't have a list of Newfoundland motels but I knew I could get the numbers from telephone information. I knew for certain he was in Port Aux Basques. In a matter of minutes I was armed with the names and numbers of three motels. Paulette sat silently as I punched in the numbers and got him on the third try. I knew his voice inflections so well, I could hear he wasn't sober.

"I don't know much yet, Michel, but I know you've been cheating on me," I said without preamble. There was a brief pause.

"What?" he said.

"How do you plan to get out of this mess?"

"I'm not in any mess, Denise."

"You are. You sure the hell are."

"Who've you been talking to?" I could hear him lighting a cigarette.

"It doesn't matter because I've just started talking."

"I don't know what you're talking about."

"You don't know what I'm talking about?"

"No."

"I'm talking about women."

Again there was a pause.

"What women?"

"How about Virginia?"

"Who?"

"Virginia. You know her?"

"Never heard of her. Where'd you get that name?"

"I got it—" *I* was fumbling for a cigarette. "I got it from a list of women I...I've got right here on the kitchen table. You don't know her?"

"No. I don't know anybody by the name of Virginia."

"I don't know her either, Michel. Which is funny, because I guess she lives pretty near us. I guess she's about the age of our children but she's married now."

"That's crazy."

"Yeah, you're right. You know what I'm going to do, Michel? I'm going to start making phone calls to the women I've got on my list and I won't quit until I find one who's willing to tell me the truth."

There was another pause. I glanced up at Paulette and I must have looked desperate. I was fighting now to keep myself under control. I actually heard Michel take a swallow of something, probably beer.

"Go ahead," he said. "Call anybody you want. Make a fool out of yourself."

I hung up.

"What are you going to do?" Paulette asked.

I flipped through the phone book and sure enough, there was the number. A young woman answered.

"I'm Denise Poirier," I said immediately. "I don't believe we've met."

"I...I don't know." Her voice was small and it almost stopped me. This might have been my own daughter.

"Maybe you know Michel Poirier."

"Michel Poirier."

"You know him?"

"I think so."

I looked across at Paulette.

"Did you go out with him?"

"Michel Poirier? He's older than my dad."

"Listen, my dear. I know this was all before you got married. All I'm asking is, did you go out with him?"

"No. Never."

I must have slumped a bit in my chair because Paulette reached across the table and touched my arm. I put the phone back to my ear.

"Victoria, listen. I need somebody's help, somebody who knows first hand. The truth is, my husband's been cheating on me—my husband I trusted totally all these years of my life—he's been cheating on me but I can't accuse him without proof. I've heard this rumour about you and him and if there's any chance that rumour is true and you could find it in your heart to help me out, I'd never blame you. You were a young girl, just a girl. Are you there?"

"Yes."

I gave her my phone number

"Think of the dilemma I'm in and please call me back if you change your mind. I'll be here."

For some reason I started thinking about all those Sunday afternoons I'd sat at home while Michel was at the bootlegger's. The women there had such a reputation, I hated him going. I hated it but I said nothing. What was I thinking?

"What are you thinking now?" Paulette asked me. I looked up.

"I was on my way to work one morning and I was having a cigarette," I remembered. "When I butted it out before going in, I noticed another butt in the ashtray with bright red lipstick on it. Du Maurier. I don't smoke Du Maurier."

Paulette said nothing.

"I remember how he and I used to go for long walks at night before my legs got bad. After that, he kept on walking by himself."

"Maybe better to forget it," Paulette said.

"Half way through his walk he'd call me from a payphone. You know what I was thinking? I was thinking, 'Boy, that man loves me.'"

I stopped to light another cigarette.

"Now I see he was just giving himself some cover."

The phone rang. I took a drag on the cigarette and picked up the receiver. It was the girl, Victoria.

"I talked it over with my husband," she said, then stopped. I could hear something that might have been weeping. She was apparently struggling to compose herself. "He says you deserve to know the truth."

"What's the truth?"

She spilled her guts. She had succumbed to his charms but it seemed she knew about a lot of women who'd been involved with him. She didn't go into much detail.

"You should leave him," she concluded. "He doesn't love you," she added with a sort of fierce emphasis and then, as a sort of afterthought, "He's a pig."

I thought, that's my husband she's talking about. I sat still a long minute. I could hear the girl sniffling softly on the other end of the line.

I said. "I want to thank you. What you've done here took courage and honesty. I appreciate it."

She didn't say anything and I hung up, then immediately picked up the phone again and started punching in the Newfoundland number. I saw poor Paulette's eyes were wide, like she'd gone to see a light comedy and then chose some sad romance but ended up in the front row of a horror movie.

"Who gave you the right to exploit thirty years of my precious life?" I shouted into the phone. "Who said it was okay to treat me like trash, with no respect, when you were totally aware of my values, when you *knew* that was the one and only thing I could never cope with? How could you sleep at night?"

Nothing he said registered. In fact, I couldn't have told you much of what I said myself, even ten minutes later. I do remember the anger boiled out of me in a fevered torrent, like the vomit that had released me from the drug the night before: fierce and hot and protective.

"You know what you are?" I screamed near the end. "You

know what you are? You're a *stranger!*"

I slammed down the phone and looked at Paulette. Then my heart broke at last.

170

A Late Departure

n his return trip from Newfoundland to North Sydney, Michel was so drunk he couldn't stand. It would have been a two-hour drive home from the ferry. The security personnel couldn't ignore the situation and took him to the North Star Inn in Sydney. From there he disappeared. I eventually got word he was at the Cape Breton Regional Hospital.

When I'd inherited the house from Normand, I'd had it put in both Michel's name and my own. I woke up one morning a day or two after the revelation and decided that I would be the sole owner. I went immediately to a lawyer and had the papers drawn up but of course I needed Michel's signature. In a lonely blur of disgust and disappointment, I wasn't sure I was fit to make decisions. Gilles and Michelle were away. I called Wilfred and then walked around the house for two days until he arrived. We talked late into the night, with me doing the talking—ranting rather—and Wilfred listening. The following morning, he drove me to Sydney.

We met at the Cape Breton Regional Hospital behind closed doors: Wilfred, Michel, me and a man whom I assumed was a security guard. Michel kept his head down, looked nervous and sad. His hands were shaking but so were mine. I passed him a pen and the papers

"Sign this," I said.

He looked up at me.

"It's the deed to the house you're losing," I said.

He signed. I picked up the paper and Wilfred and I left.

When we got back home as soon as we stepped in the door the phone rang—some kind of lawyer representing hospital patients. He said Michel's signature was worth nothing because he'd signed under duress and under a lot of medication. I just laughed at him and banged down the phone.

The next morning we got up and went through the house, filled garbage bag after garbage bag with Michel's stuff. When we were finished, the basement rec room was full of bags. Wilfred had to go back home but friends kept calling and popping in and out, bringing me food I couldn't eat. I was overwhelmed by tiredness, surrounded by others but completely alone.

One evening after supper, Michel showed up with his brother. He'd been discharged from the hospital.

"Your stuff's in the rec room," I said. "Take it and get out."

One of his brothers owned an apartment in Cheticamp and he moved in there. Every other day he called, crying to come back home. He hated it at the apartment. He had the gall to tell me he loved me and missed me so much. To my torment he added his own.

I wandered from room to room in what had been

Normand's house and once had been our house.

"Maybe getting out of here would be good for you," Gilles said one day on the phone. He was away a lot and suggested I let Michel move back into the house temporarily. I agreed and for some time I lived in Gilles' place in Petit Étang, at the edge of the forest. There, truly alone, I could consider my fate. Over the years, as I'd come to understand that my peripheral vascular disease was advanced and chronic and that, far from getting better, I'd be getting ever so gradually worse, I'd determined to enjoy every day to the fullest. There was no prospect of that now.

I missed the sea, the harbour, the bustle of traffic. Every day or so, I drove down to Cheticamp, where I discovered myself to be in the limelight. Everyone in the village had always known, it seemed—everyone except me and my children. I sat through sombre afternoon coffees with friends and in-laws. Why hadn't they told me? They would look at one another. They'd known all about my health. They knew how much I valued my relationship with Michel. The shock might have killed me, they said. They were right. It was killing me now.

I ate almost nothing and smoked all day. I vomited often and developed diarrhea, lost weight until my skin hung off my bones. Dr. Aucoin gave me his phone number and told me to call on him day or night if I experienced chest pain I couldn't control with the nitro.

The first few months passed and the haze began to lift. I knew I'd survive. I knew I'd steer my mind back to normal. I knew I'd persevere. But I knew I couldn't do it faced with the tide of sympathy from the kind people of Cheticamp. My only choice was to totally erase from my mind not only

Michel but all of my life in that village that had been my life.

I obtained a legal separation in October and decided to move to Montreal, where I'd visited my brother Ronald so often. Gilles helped me make the arrangements whenever he was home from sea. I can't say precisely why I changed my mind.

Sydney is a small city but it's the only city on Cape Breton. "I'll just go there awhile," I thought. "Then I'll go far away for good."

My last afternoon, an October afternoon, I drove the jeep up to the National Park along the roads that Bernice and I had so often followed on our bikes those many years before. As I drove I looked up at the mountains, up to the east, where the wilderness of forest began. Near the top I parked and sat for some time, looking off to the west, across the harbour and the island to the ocean, then I drove back down to Cheticamp.

The day in 1958 they paved the main road—what we now call the Cabot Trail—that had been a big day for me, a ten-year-old. I'd sat myself on the front veranda and watched the machinery bury the dirt road I'd known all my life. Then— the wonder of it—they'd painted a white line down the middle.

I drove up our old street and passed the church. A motel now stood between our house and Georgina's. At the bottom of the street, P'tit Joe and Adelaide had owned the Acadian Inn, which had accommodated the few tourists who came that way. P'tit Joe and Adelaide sold to the Aucoins and the Inn eventually burned to the ground. Hotels and restaurants had sprung up to replace it many times over as features of the new, very up-to-date Cheticamp. Also gone from that corner was the old community hall that Cheticantins had used for meetings and concerts—torn down just in time for my teen-age years and replaced with pride by Le Centre Acadien. Outside Le Centre, the boys would spend their winter nights flooding the rink for hockey and on frozen afternoons we'd all skate around to the sound of tinny waltzes. The building was still there, with its hall and bowling alley and pool tables, but the rink was gone. I drove past slowly and glanced at the window where Bernice and I had once shared fries and our opinions of Michel Poirier.

I turned up the driveway to where my school had been in the old OLA convent, now vanished, and I passed by the Sacred Heart Hospital which was attached to the nuns' residence. The old hospital too was gone, replaced by a modern facility. The nuns of Cheticamp, like all the rest of Cheticamp, had to come to terms with the world.

And then I wasn't sure where to go. The grassy fields and scattered old houses were busy, suburban-looking streets now inhabited by busy, suburban-looking people, many of them speaking English. The farmers were gone and the smell of new-mown hay had gone with them. I sat with the motor running by the side of the street. I lit a cigarette.

Finally I turned around and went down further on the harbour, where the lobster factory had stood. The fishery is the one part of old Cheticamp that was still there—had grown in fact. I stopped and made an effort to picture myself

crawling into the lobster bin and after a minute I could actually recall the crunch of shells under my feet, the squeals of
hungry kids waiting for me to pass out the feast.

"Pass them, Denise! Hurry!"

"Okay! Wait!"

"Hurry, Denise!"

I knew I had tears rolling down my cheeks but I couldn't
help laughing to myself. Those damn lobster bodies had tast-
ed good.

The harbour was quiet now and the island across the water
slept in the afternoon sunlight. I looked up and down the
highway as I had thousands of times, saw how it still twisted
away in either direction, following the sea and flanked by the
wooded hills of Cape Breton.

The next morning I turned onto that highway and drove
out of Cheticamp. It would never be my home again.

Afterword

I f you follow the Cabot Trail from Cheticamp right around the big island of Cape Breton, you'll come to a small city on the far eastern side and facing out to the North Atlantic Ocean. This is Sydney, Nova Scotia. It was at one time a working place of steel and coal but that's passed now and Sydney has become a quiet backwater whose sons and daughters often leave to find work in more prosperous cities. Yet with each passing summer, thousands of others find their way by plane and car and cruise ship from almost everywhere to this seaside outpost at the eastern end of Canada. I suppose they come because they want to experience what the turmoil of the centuries has left as evidence: the people of Cape Breton—the Highland Scots, the Acadian French, the Irish, the Empire Loyalists, the English, the African Canadians and even eastern Europeans.

I ended up in Sydney too, not as a tourist but as a woman in self-imposed exile who didn't want to leave the land she knew. After her divorce, my daughter Michelle had moved with my grandson Matthew to take up a position at the hospital in Sydney, so the town shone like a beacon for me as

I fled my village past. I arrived with only my computer and my photo albums, from which I'd purged anything touched by Michel. I got rid of all my clothes and bought a new wardrobe he'd never see. I got rid of my gold jewellery and started wearing silver. I lost money trading my almost new Ford Explorer for another car because I was certain Michel had enjoyed other women in the Ford. The dealer suggested instead that they just clean it for me but I refused.

I took an apartment in Michelle's building and settled un-easily into apartment life. Little Matthew visited me every day and this proved a godsend. We set up a small tent in the living room and often camped there together. When my son Gilles returned from sea he'd share the apartment with me. Still numb, I was nonetheless grateful for the love of my family. Every day I made myself go out to a grocery store or a movie or a restaurant or the library and even to a counsellor. I passed people on the street and I relished how they passed me without a glance. No sad smiles. No pity.

Towards the end of January, 1999, the telephone rang at suppertime. I looked at the caller ID on the screen and hesitated. I knew no Gerard Cormier.

"Denise?" A man's voice.

"Yes?"

"This is Gerard Cormier. I'm a friend of Joe Moroze. I'm calling to see if you're interested in meeting me for a coffee at Tim Horton's. Joe gave me your name and phone number. We could meet there at 8:00 if you like."

"Joe gave you my number?"

My cousin Juliette had married Joe Moroze and they lived in Sydney now. It was difficult for me to do my housecleaning and Juliette would come over to help on her days off.

"Yeah. Joe said we ought to have coffee, you and me. There's that Tims on George Street."

"At eight o'clock."

"Would that be alright?"

"Yeah, it would."

Gerard Cormier and I met at the Tim Hortons on George Street, Sydney and were married the same year, two days after Christmas, at the Ramada Motel. He was a proper Cape Bretoner, Gerard. He spoke little French but his parents were of French-speaking Acadian stock from the Cheticamp area and of course Mama knew of them

and approved. We liked the same movies and the same music and we each had a son and daughter. Now for the first time I discovered what it was to be respected, to say nothing of being showered with flowers and Christmas gifts that would leave me in tears of surprise and gratitude. We talked openly and endlessly and only a few months passed before I realized I knew him better than I'd ever known Michel.

Today our house in Westmount, Nova Scotia overlooks the harbour and on the other side is the centre of Sydney. At night, from our living room window, we can look past the masts of the yacht club and watch the lights of the town play on the water of the harbour. The harbour leads out to the sea.

Mama died at the age of 84 on January 18, 2004 and my last link to Cheticamp was finally broken.

My brother Wilfred and his wife Marie France retired and still live in Shediac, New Brunswick. His health is not the best but he gets by with the help of medication and a defibrillator.

My brother Ronald retired from Montreal and now lives with my daughter Michelle about a three minute drive from our house in Sydney.

Georgina moved to Halifax when she was young. She still lives there by herself, working for Scotia Investments Ltd. as a benefits manager. She looks after the pension plans and group insurance programs for about 2,000 employees of eight companies owned by the company.

Bernice settled in Toronto, then retired to St. Joseph du Moine, where she lives with her husband.

Claudie Aucoin still lives and works in Cheticamp.

My son Gilles married Shauna and they have a six–year-old son, Mark. Gilles is

captain of the *Thebaud Sea*, a ship engaged in offshore construction in the Persian Gulf.

My daughter Michelle works as an MRI technologist at the Cape Breton Regional Hospital. Her son Matthew now works out west. His aim is to become a millionaire.

Michel Poirier married again, a much younger woman. He's divorced now for a second time and shares custody of their seven-year-old son.

I n March of 2001, the little bit of walking I'd been able to do came to a complete stop. One evening, I looked up at Gerard as we sat together.

"I think it's another occlusion in my right leg," I said. "I can tell."

He nodded. "Well, let's see. They already know you're bull-headed and questioning, these doctors, so they won't be surprised to see you. Let's get it checked out. Maybe they can do another repair."

Dr. Murdock Smith was my miraculously patient family doctor and Dr. Smith referred me to Rex Dunn, a cardiovascular surgeon. Dr. Dunn ordered a arteriogram that confirmed my suspicions.

"Let's not give up, Denise," he said. "I'm fairly confident

we can repair this with an angioplasty."

"What have I got to lose?"

"Nothing, really."

The angioplasty was a success and I could slowly and painfully walk again. That what I'd been doing for years, so it came easily enough.

I went back to see Dr. Dunn one afternoon that spring. It was a good day, with only a few clouds in the way of the sun. My heart was light and easy, fortified with gratitude that I was on my feet again. Dr. Dunn sat with me in his office for a long while as he went patiently through my files and reviewed everything. My abdominal  aorta was as narrow as it could be and still function at all. Some of my leg arteries—he called them "threads"—could not even be seen on an x-ray. When he was done he put down his pen and looked at me. By now I was familiar with his expression: not smiling but not grave either.

"So an old expert like you understands this perfectly well," he said. "I know that. From what we can see now, your peripheral vascular disease is just too advanced for me to do any more repairs. This was the last one."

"I do understand perfectly well. Believe me, I do. I've had a lot of practice."

He smiled. "You have."

I stood up. "I know I'm a handful," I said. "It's just that I have to be."

He extended his hand.

"Denise," he said. "Make me a promise."

"Of course."

"Promise me you'll go home and be happy."

"I'm an old expert at that too," I said. "But thanks for your skill—and your honesty."

He nodded. "Goodbye, Denise—and good luck."

"I've had some," I said.

I walked out of his office and onto Glenwood Street. The sky had completely cleared now and the sun was out and warm. Just as I'd expected.

Denise Cormier
Sydney, Nova Scotia, 2011

Denise Cormier can be reached by e-mail at
mat3926@eastlink.ca

ENCOMPASS EDITIONS is a young publishing house, founded in 2009 and based in Kingston, Ontario, Canada but dedicated to providing access to traditional publishing to a wider spectrum of writers than is often the case—writers in the United States, Canada, the United Kingdom and the European Union.

Although Encompass does not accept unsolicited manuscripts, the company relies upon several agents who work closely with writers at every level of experience. This policy permits Encompass to focus on what it does best: publish books good to read.

You can visit the Encompass website at www.EncompassEditions.com or contact editor Robert Buckland at words@encompasseditions.com